The 22 Non-Negotiable
Laws of Wellness

Also by Greg Anderson

The Cancer Conqueror

The Triumphant Patient

*50 Essential Things to Do When the
Doctor Says It's Cancer*

Healing Wisdom

The 22 Non-Negotiable Laws of Wellness

Feel, Think, and Live Better
Than You Ever Thought Possible

Greg Anderson

HarperSanFrancisco
An Imprint of HarperCollins*Publishers*

HarperCollins Web Site: http://www.harpercollins.com
HarperCollins®, 📖®, and HarperSanFrancisco™ are trademarks of HarperCollins Publishers Inc.

FIRST HARPERCOLLINS PAPERBACK EDITION PUBLISHED IN 1996

Library of Congress Cataloging-in-Publication Data:

Anderson, Greg.
The 22 non-negotiable laws of wellness: feel, think, and live better than you ever thought possible/Greg Anderson. —1st ed.
    ISBN 0-06-251235-8 (cloth)
    ISBN 0-06-251238-2 (pbk.)
    1. Health.   2. Mental health.   3. Conduct of life.
    I. Title.   II. Title: Twenty-two non-negotiable laws of wellness.
RA 776.5.A628 1995
613—dc20   94-42770

96 97 98 99 00 RRD(H) 10 9 8 7 6 5 4 3 2 1

For my wife, Linda,
and our daughter, Erica,
and
my friends and mentors,
George and Mary Jane Leader

Contents

Acknowledgments

My heartfelt thanks go to the hundreds of people who have allowed me to share their healing journeys. To the members of the Cancer Conquerors Foundation, thank-you for inspiring me with your stories of living the well life. I felt a closeness to each of you as I wrote.

Thanks, too, to the residents of Country Meadows Assisted Living Communities. You've taught me about truly living. Whenever I have cited a story of yours, it's a composite drawn from the real stories but with no resemblance to any one person's experience. In all cases I hope the dignity, integrity, and courage of each person has been preserved.

My gratitude to my family—my wife, Linda, and our daughter, Erica—for allowing me to share some of our experiences. And thank-you for your support and patience when I'd lock myself in the study, writing, between trips away from home.

George and Mary Jane Leader, I am so deeply grateful to each of you. Your belief in and constant support of my work is a precious gift. I can't express how much you mean to me and how our shared experience has given joy to my life.

To my friends at Harper San Francisco: Tom Grady, you grasped the vision of this project immediately; Caroline Pincus, your editorial touch is exceptional; Robin Seaman, your enthusiasm is contagious; and Clayton Carlson, you've never been afraid of a new idea. Thank-you all.

To God, for life, after it looked like mine on this planet was about to end, my deepest loving gratitude. Thank-you for giving me the opportunity to serve.

Introduction

Wellness is one of the greatest and most powerful words in the English language. Unfortunately, it is also one of the least understood. But start putting this word into your vocabulary and the concepts it entails into your life. Wellness is one of the most important ideas of our time.

After two years of fruitless debate between the U.S. Congress and the president, support for government health-care reform has dissipated. A Gallup Organization poll explained the results of the debate: fewer people now consider governmental action desirable as a solution to our health-care problems. In contrast, Americans believe individuals must take greater responsibility for controlling their own health-care costs.

Indeed, 85 percent of the Gallup Poll respondents believe their physical well-being depends on how well they care for themselves. That is the heart of wellness, I believe it is our country's only real and lasting means of true health-care reform. This approach to health care, and to life, is really the only viable option. It is based on the truth that we as individuals make the single most powerful contribution to our health and well-being. Not the doctor. Not prescription medications. We do. Herein lies power!

Wellness is the complete integration of body, mind, and spirit—the realization that everything we do, think, feel, and believe has an effect on our state of well-being.

Wellness is a choice, a decision we make to move toward optimal health and maximum life.

Wellness is a process—an awareness that there is no end point but that health and happiness are always possible in the present moment, here and now.

Wellness is not a "medical fix" but a way of living—a lifestyle sensitive and responsive to all the dimensions of body, mind, and spirit; an approach to life we each design to achieve our highest potential for well-being now and forever.

Medicine deals with one dimension, the body. Old self-help ideas dealt with one dimension, typically the mind. Wellness involves an all-inclusive paradigm shift. Its practice encompasses six major life areas—the physical, emotional, social, intellectual, vocational, and spiritual spheres. Wellness is not a piecemeal approach; it involves the total you!

Traditional medicine finds a problem—a symptom—and treats it. The goal is to neutralize symptoms, to return to a point of no discernible illness. This is the *disease model* of medicine. Preventive medicine, trumpeted by an increasing number in the medical community, is also based on the disease model. The goal is the same: no discernible illness.

Wellness strives for a new standard. No matter what our state of health, wellness calls for continuing improvement and self-renewal in all areas of life. Wellness seeks more than the absence of illness; it searches for new levels of excellence. Beyond any disease-free neutral point, wellness dedicates its efforts to our total well-being—in body, mind, and spirit.

The 22 Non-Negotiable Laws of Wellness distills more than a decade of experience in the field of health enhancement and life enrichment into a set of basic laws that govern success and failure in the pursuit of total wellness. This book describes the fundamental rules of the wellness pursuit.

But who says so? How can one guy without an M.D. or Ph.D. behind his name discover what thousands of others have overlooked? After all, there are many sophisticated wellness practitioners and academics. Why do I think I can lay down the laws?

The answer is simple. Since 1984, I have based my life on them. That was the year I was diagnosed with metastatic lung cancer and told that I had thirty days to live. Conventional medicine could do nothing more for me. These laws brought me back from the brink of death. In the decade since, I have dedicated myself to understanding and teaching them. Those are credentials, I submit, that make for valid authority.

I ask you to open your mind and spirit to these laws. You're more familiar with their content than you might believe.

Be challenged. Learn. Then do. There's no substitute for the commitment to implement. I hope my own journey and those of literally tens of thousands of patients I have learned from and shared with will help you attain greater wellness. You may find some of the laws challenging, but keep in mind that they are all true guideposts for living. I wish you well on your own journey to wellness.

Greg Anderson

Part One

_____

The Universal Laws

1

The Law of
Esprit

The joy you feel is life!

Many people believe that the basic issues in wellness are (1) disciplining ourselves to eat well and (2) exercising regularly.

Not true.

The single overriding objective in wellness is creating constant personal renewal where we recognize and act on the truth that each day is a miraculous gift and our job is to untie the ribbons.

That's the Law of Esprit: living life with joy.

Joy—the emotion evoked by well-being. Delight. Bliss. Genuine happiness. True wellness is the ability to generate a joyful stance toward life on a daily basis.

The practice of wellness carries with it the exceptional promise that we can know an *esprit*, a deep satisfaction, in all areas of our life experience. The goal of this profound personal work: a life of joy. Knowing the Law of Esprit.

If we have widely variable willpower and fight a constant battle over food and exercise, then our wellness strategy has probably been faulty from the start. We have violated the first law of wellness—esprit.

If life is a constant battle against weight gain, a herculean effort of keeping fit, a career filled with struggle, a marriage that is toxic, we have missed wellness. We have missed it because we have missed the joy. The Law of Esprit has not been honored.

The Law of Esprit recognizes that what we wish and expect governs the response we get. For example, people who consider how to improve their physical, mental, and spiritual well-being every day for the balance of their lives immediately begin to see three values emerge:

1. *satisfaction,* since for them life becomes primarily a pleasant experience;
2. *creativity,* which keeps life interesting and makes us want more of it;
3. *wisdom,* which is the collective reward of the well life.

People who focus on how difficult their physical, mental, and spiritual circumstances are tend to see like values emerge—dissatisfaction, despair, and dissonance.

The Law of Esprit implies that we want as much satisfaction, creativity, and wisdom as possible. The result: joy! And this joy extends to every area of life—our body, our mind, our relationships, our personal growth, our sense of meaning and purpose, and our experience of being a spiritually rooted creation.

Tremendous!

Exciting!

Where do we find this esprit? It's everywhere. We discover it in the mystery of a sunrise—thanking God we're alive to enjoy it. Or in the magic that's a raindrop—thrilled that nature nourishes all creation with plenty.

Looking deeper, we find esprit in the touch of a caring hand, the concern of a loving mate, the companionship of a close friend. "We've been buddies over fifty years," shared Edythe as she hugged her friend Marie, who was now living in a nursing home. "That's truly special."

We find esprit in accomplishments that satisfy. "Look at this collection of birds my father made," said Vanessa as she toured me through their home. "He is at his happiest when he can carve the wood and paint the details of the feathers."

Esprit suffuses the participants who help achieve a shared goal. "We did it!" is proof that cooperation is spelled with two letters: *w-e*. And in that participation comes joy.

Esprit is an intense love affair with life. It is making the most of now, enjoying what is at hand, as we go along.

Esprit is shifting our awareness to look for the joys that come in small, precious packages. Once we discover those joys, it is then our privilege to make the most of them. Our focus moves away from looking for the big packages of joy, which are few and far between. Instead, we become aware of life as it is, here and now, and we celebrate.

"Some people," wrote the poet Walt Whitman, "are so much sunshine to the square inch." That's esprit—

the person who seems to radiate the rays of the sun from within.

No megashift need take place. Esprit blossoms gently. The inner music begins to crescendo, like a happy band of musicians marching down the street.

Does esprit mean no more tears? Of course not. But it does mean that life can be complete, though perhaps never the same, after the loss that comes with tears. Even in the midst of those tears, esprit can be born as we recall the memories of joyous days gone by.

Esprit belongs at work. On the job it comes when we put forth all our powers in a wave of inspiration and creative joy, when we recognize that an organization that serves others is fulfilling its highest purpose.

Esprit is found in relationships where our focus is on developing a heart that is aglow with love for all we meet.

Let us be about setting high standards for life, love, creativity, and wisdom. If our expectations in these areas are low, we are not likely to experience wellness. Setting high standards makes every day and every decade worth looking forward to.

So the first Law of Wellness is esprit—a recognition that joy in life, not length of life, is the marker by which all wellness is measured.

Does that mean that if one's life lacks esprit, he or she is doomed to languish forever? Not necessarily. Fortunately, there are other laws.

2

The Law of
Personal
Accountability

If it's going to be,
it's up to me.

—*Robert H. Schuller*

2

The Law of
Personal
Accountability

If it's going to be,
it's up to me.

—*Robert H. Schuller*

Most people think wellness is a question of eating your vegetables, taking a daily walk, and having good genes. In the long run, they figure, "my genes will determine my health and my life. My efforts are secondary."

That belief is an illusion. The Law of Personal Accountability states that it is *we*—yes, you and I—who are responsible, first and foremost, for our own wellness.

Ted is a friend who works for one of America's most prominent television personalities. His job is to locate funding for various programs and productions. The job means lots of travel, entertaining in fine restaurants, and high-powered, high-stakes contacts all over the country.

Three years into the job, Ted starts to put on weight. Lots of weight. Soon he carries forty pounds more than his target. I try to talk exercise. "Travel makes it tough," says Ted. "I'm always on the road. Face it: it's difficult to exercise."

We talk diet—over lunch at one of his favorite gourmet restaurants. Ted proudly points out he is ordering salad. But he also asks for two side orders of blue-cheese dressing! "Don't eat that," I protest. "It's full of fat." "Come on! My God, Greg," replies Ted, "it's a salad."

I talk meditation, which was such an important part of my survival from a terminal-cancer diagnosis. But Ted can't hear "Calm your mind. Nurture your spirit." His idea of using the mind to heal is just to "think positive."

Early in 1990, Ted starts to experience chest pains. Just an occasional jab at first. Then more frequent jolts. "Probably just heartburn," he says. Ted begins to worry. But he is too busy to see a doctor.

Finally, during an overnight red-eye from Los Angeles to New York, the pain becomes unbearable. There is a doctor on board who attends him during the flight. He tells Ted he's on the verge of a heart attack.

Ted is frightened. He goes directly from the airport to a doctor.

The physician easily recognizes and confirms the symptoms of heart trouble and sends him that morning to see a cardiologist. After an exam of but a few minutes, the cardiologist's words to Ted are: "You're a walking time bomb. Your heart could explode any minute. We must do bypass surgery immediately."

Amazingly, Ted agrees. Here is a cautious man who always weighs his decisions carefully. Yet in this instance, he doesn't once question the directive of the surgeon. It's open-heart bypass surgery—today!

Fortunately, the surgery goes well. The cardiologist puts him on a low-fat diet and prescribes a program of daily exercise. I am able to convince him that some daily quiet time of prayer and meditation will contribute to his well-being, too. Ted complies.

The weight comes off almost immediately. He looks better than he has in fifteen years. People comment about his renewed youthful appearance. A real smile returns his face. We talk about him cutting back at work and even changing jobs.

But Ted can't give up his position. He goes back— at first, for just a couple of days a week. Then a trip is squeezed in. No rough travel schedule, mind you. An easy visit, back the next evening.

You guessed it. It hasn't been three months before Ted is back at work full-time. He is planning for the fall programs. Today, he lives from one adrenaline rush to another. "It's all so intoxicating," he smiles. How true.

Ted's weight is back. His exercise is sporadic. Cocktails now stretch to three or four before evening meals. Meditation? Forget it. The travel schedule is again jammed as he hurries from meeting to meeting, always in search of the big deal.

Now when I ask Ted about his health, he comments, "When my number is up, it's up. There's not much I can do." Not much he can do? Not true! As educated, experienced, and sophisticated as Ted is, he is not wellness wise. He can't comprehend—he won't comprehend—the implications of the Law of Personal Accountability.

Two wellness conclusions we know to be true:

1. *Behaviors contribute to illness or wellness.* Our choices regarding food, alcohol, tobacco, exercise, and drugs have profound effects on the development of disease and our potential for recovery from disease.

The list of examples is long. The link between wine, cheese, chocolate, and migraine headaches is widely acknowledged. Diabetics can control the amount of insulin they require by care and attention to proper diet and nutrition. Exercise can help rebuild a person's entire cardiovascular system following heart disease.

In case after case, behaviors within our control influence, for better or worse, both the onset of and the recovery from a wide variety of illnesses.

2. *Responses, both emotional and spiritual, can lead to physical changes. Prevention* magazine, in a widely quoted study, reported that 90 percent of all physical problems have psychological roots. That may sound like a gross exaggeration. In fact, ongoing research indicates that it is probably a conservative estimate.

Your physiological state is determined in large part by the way you respond to the circumstances of your life. A calm response generates "soothing" biochemicals. An angry or fearful high-stress response generates toxic biochemicals. Over a prolonged period, unchecked psychological stress can contribute to illness by creating physiological turmoil.

Study after study links our response to stress with a long list of "dis-eases." Thousands of asthma sufferers obtain immediate relief by using basic relaxation techniques. The same is true for people dealing with chest pains related to heart disease. Arthritis sufferers who go through therapy to address and resolve issues of harbored anger and resentment find dramatic relief from their symptoms. Even children with problems—from colicky babies and bed-wetting three-year-olds to kindergartners with frequent stomachaches and sore throats—are often responding to major sources of stress in their environment, says Harold Jackson, a Greenville, South Carolina, pediatrician.

The Law of Personal Accountability shouts that we have the ability to choose both our behaviors and our responses! It's more than stress management; it's personal choice.

The power of this law is stupendous, its implications massive.

On the negative side, if we neglect giving mindful attention to our behaviors and responses, we will surely deteriorate physically, emotionally, and spiritually.

The good news is that this coin has two sides. Although our inattention can contribute to our lack of total well-being, we also have the power to choose positive behaviors and responses.

In that choice, we change our every experience of life!

The principle of choice embodied in the Law of Personal Accountability is one of the most misunderstood concepts in modern America. People say, "But you're blaming people for becoming sick." Not so!

The Law of Personal Accountability isn't about blaming anyone for anything. The law simply points out that our behaviors and responses, no matter what the circumstance, are under our control.

I've personally seen the law cut both ways. After one of my cancerous lungs was removed, I slipped right back into old behaviors and responses—lots of high-fat fast food, little exercise, and a workaholic life.

While I make no claims that my example constitutes valid medical research, I personally believe that my negative behaviors and responses greatly contributed to my forced return to the hospital, where a cancer recurrence was discovered. As a result, in December 1984 a surgeon told me I had thirty days to live.

There's nothing like bad news to get your attention. I felt I had two ways to go. One was to give in to the despair and prepare to die. The other, with no promise of success, was to decide to fully participate in an effort to get well.

I chose the latter. Today, with perfect hindsight, I see that I had a vitally important role to play. I firmly believe that changes in my diet and exercise made a real difference. I knew no stress-management techniques and needed to learn from the beginning. I started. Over a period of weeks, I became aware that I had to change spiritually. I began.

People often ask me, "When did you realize you were going to live more than thirty days?" My answer has always been, "On the thirty-first day!" Once I began to implement the Law of Personal Accountability, it was just a matter of weeks before I started to improve. My spirits lifted. My appetite improved. The pain became more manageable. I allowed myself some thoughts about getting well again.

I looked deeply into my responses toward life, especially into my need for power and approval. Why was I putting myself through emotional torture with the silly need to always be right? Why did I always see other people as a threat? My responses were creating this personal inner warfare. Crazy!

And I started to seriously explore my spiritual self. By some standards, I was on track. I followed the "rules" reasonably well. But I discovered I wasn't spiritual, I was religious. And there's a big difference. More on that in a later law.

As I explored my behaviors and responses, I began to understand what a pivotal role I played. This same power of choice is at work in all of us, no matter what our age, no matter what our physical or mental condition. There are no exceptions. We may not always be aware of it, but it is there. And we are accountable for being aware of its potential in our lives. Will we use this power for our good or toward our demise?

It's the Law of Personal Accountability. We have the ability to develop an awareness of our own behavior and responses, physically, emotionally, and spiritually. The law requires us to make these life choices courageously, even in the midst of uncertainty. We have considerable power to create the life and the health we want rather than just reacting to life's events.

Do you believe you have that power? Probably not? But it's true. And what you and I believe does matter.

Wellness is not solely a question of genetics or even of diet and exercise. It's first an awareness of our considerable potential and then an understanding of our accountability for its use.

Sound frightening? Fear not! There are some other important laws that take the sharp edges off this concept. Just know for now that we can change our physical well-being. We can choose our emotions. We can find meaning and purpose in life. And as we do, the Law of Personal Accountability becomes a point of power, not a personal tyrant.

3

The Law of
Unity

The part can never be well
unless the whole is well.

—Plato

Oh, the miracle of it all! There is far more to life than what is physically obvious.

Conventional wisdom, most notably the traditional model of medical science, has it that we are primarily physical beings. We are cells, and groups of cells, physical and material in nature.

Others believe the mind holds all the answers. You are what you think. Your mind has unlimited power. Your attitude determines your altitude, some claim. The message: we are primarily mental beings. Motivational psychologists live in luxury spinning this tale.

Still others want us to consider ourselves essentially spiritual. We are souls, supernatural beings, endowed with spirit. This spirit gives life and is life, now and forever. Our spiritual leaders comfort the afflicted and afflict the comfortable with this idea every week.

In truth, we are body, mind, *and* spirit. We are three distinct entities. Yet these entities are inseparable. One. Whole.

The awareness that body, mind, and spirit constantly and powerfully interact has significant implications for the way we view illness, treat disease, and conduct our lives. Wellness encompasses this entire spectrum.

Taking prescribed insulin, for example, will help control excessive amounts of sugar in the blood and urine. But the effectiveness of insulin without dietary control is limited. If diabetics regularly and joyfully exercise, they increase their chance of living a long and healthy life. Many who include a period of daily meditation have found that the symptoms of diabetes decrease even more. Adopt a forgiving, grateful, loving, more spiritual stance toward life, and the physical response is often astounding.

What's at work is one of the most powerful truths in wellness: the Law of Unity.

How exciting!

We are more than a group of cells. Our minds are not only in our brain but also in every cell of our bodies. Our spirit—and yes, we each have a powerful spirit—does not reside in a symbolic heart but suffuses every tiny corner of our being, and beyond.

There is constant interaction between body, mind, and spirit. We are always making and remolding ourselves on all three levels. We are forever hiding or releasing our great potentials for enhancing our health and well-being.

The perpetual communication between the body, mind, and spirit implies that if we address only one of these elements we may not be able to achieve the best possible results.

The Law of Unity tells us we can no longer separate body, mind, and spirit. When we do so, our analysis no longer conforms to the truth. Our new understanding takes us beyond our previous beliefs of separateness and asks, "Where does body end and mind start? Where does mind find its limits and spirit become reality?" The line of division between the three is very fine, indeed. It quickly blurs. We need a new analysis.

My wife, Linda, and I received a call that our daughter, eight years old at the time, had fallen while visiting the public library with the neighbors. She was going down a flight of stairs, tripped, and smashed her head into a brick wall. The bleeding was profuse.

We rushed to the hospital. The scene was pandemonium. Our daughter was on an emergency-room table. Two nurses, one at our daughter's side, the other at a supply closet, shouted at full volume and frantically waved their arms, signaling to each other. Our daughter's loud cry pierced the bedlam. And the neophyte physician yelled, "Be quiet. I'm in charge," even though she couldn't get the stitches started.

Linda took one look at the situation, turned a strange shade of gray, and fainted. Out cold!

Examine this for a moment. Where does Linda's physical response of fainting originate? Is it physical?

There certainly is a physical component; she's momentarily not with us. But is this response fully triggered on the level of the body?

Or is the trigger mental? Does Linda's mind perceive the situation as overwhelming? And might that perception start a series of physiological responses that result in a temporary decrease in blood supply to the brain? That's how the emergency-room personnel explain it.

Or is the trigger spiritual? Is Linda's fainting a way of coping with a life trauma that threatens to take away her only child. Is it God's way of helping Linda to take care of herself and her own needs in the midst of a crisis?

It's a simple issue of a person fainting. But where are the demarcation points between body, mind, and spirit? The medical authorities answer quickly: the blood supply was temporarily decreased to the brain. They tell us what happened on a physical level. That explanation may be technically true, but it is not complete.

That's the Law of Unity. Body, mind, and spirit work together.

Doctors say wellness is found through medical treatment. Psychologists tell us the Holy Grail is personal introspection. Our priests and rabbis seem to think answers lie in Scripture and in ceremony.

Partial truths all. Each has only one piece of the answer. The Law of Unity demands of us a recognition that it all works together.

A vibrant balance between body, mind, and spirit makes the wellness world go round. A daily jog and salad for lunch won't get you the results you seek. All the Laws of Wellness must work together.

Part Two

The Physical Laws

4

The Law of
Physical Activity

Use it or lose it.

"I don't have time."

"It's no fun."

"I'm too tired."

"I don't like to sweat."

"I look ugly in shorts."

"I don't like the discomfort."

"The weather's bad."

"It's too much like work."

"It's boring."

You've heard them. I've used them. They're excuses—for people who don't want to exercise. You may be familiar with a few.

Even the best intentions to travel the path of wellness won't get us very far without the Law of Physical Activity. Think of it as Wellness 101.

The critical importance of exercise has been recognized for centuries. Modern studies confirming its positive influence are legion. The message is repeated in newspapers and magazines and on television. From grade schools to nursing homes, throughout our lives, the message is clear: we need to exercise! There's little room to debate the powerful Law of Physical Activity.

The list of benefits of exercise is long. Regular physical activity will

- tone muscles;
- improve your figure and posture;
- increase your energy level;
- increase your heart and lung capacity;
- prevent loss of bone density;
- relieve stress;
- burn calories and decrease—yes, decrease— appetite;
- help you avoid and more readily recover from injuries;
- help keep weight off;
- help reduce physical pain;
- brighten your mood;
- improve cognition;
- make you feel and look younger.

The Law of Physical Activity is powerful!

If the pharmaceutical industry could bottle and sell a compound that would do all these things, the product would be hailed as the greatest wonder drug of the century. It would also, no doubt, be expensive.

The Law of Physical Activity carries an important condition: the activity must be regular. The benefits of exercise can't be stored.

For years medical schools have recommended exercise three times per week. But this advice completely misses the boat. If you don't make exercise part of your daily life, chances are you won't exercise at all.

Regular daily exercise will keep your fitness level up to par. I recommend at least twenty minutes a day, each and every day.

Twenty minutes is one-seventy-second of your day. Who doesn't have twenty minutes a day? The Law of Physical Activity becomes real only by making it part of daily life.

But the Law of Physical Activity is not an easy law. Simple, yes. Easy, no.

Exercise, just like eating, means changing personal habits that over time may have become very comfortable. "That's just the way I am" is no longer a valid excuse. "I can exercise and I will exercise" is the mind-set that will serve us best.

I know. After my lung cancer diagnosis, I began to interview survivors, hoping to learn their secrets. Exercise kept coming up as a key ingredient of recovery. So I bought myself an exercise bike, a set of weights, a treadmill, and an assortment of ropes, rubber bands, and "spring things." I thought I'd put myself on the wellness track.

But the gap between "purchaser" and "user" is wide. After an initial burst of enthusiasm, my fancy equipment started to gather dust. Boxes were stacked on the treadmill. Lawn and garden tools leaned up against the exercise bike. Cobwebs actually sprouted around the barbell.

One Saturday, I finally hauled all the equipment over to a neighbor's garage sale and sold it for tens cents on the dollar. Defeated and ashamed, I knew it was the only honest thing to do.

The story doesn't stop there. The weights and exercise bike were purchased by another neighbor. This past spring he had his own garage sale. You guessed it: my prized exercise equipment changed owners again.

Despite my own and my neighbor's heroic intentions, our go-for-the-gold, world-beater attitude did not result in transforming the Law of Physical Activity into a reality for us.

So what do we do? And how can we get started implementing the Law of Physical Activity? As the Nike ad states, "Just do it!" There's more wisdom in those words than we may realize.

To get myself to exercise daily, I had to come to an understanding that moderate, less intense, less extreme activity was not only just fine; it was preferable. It would work. Forget the weights and treadmill. My new starting point was "On your mark! Get set! Walk!"

Walking was the answer. I didn't need any expensive equipment. No more complicated formulas for maximum oxygen uptake or calorie burn. I didn't even have to understand the differences between anaerobic and aerobic metabolism.

Walking! Simple. Easy. And I could do it anywhere.

All I had to do was put one foot in front of the other. I'd start slowly for the first five minutes, increase my speed for the next twenty minutes but never so fast that I was out of breath, and end slowly the last five minutes. Presto! There was my new program.

No new athletic skills were required. No court-time fees. No expensive equipment. The basic requirement was a good pair of walking shoes and my commitment to "just do it." This made sense.

I've been walking for more than eight years. I can say with integrity that I practice this program thirty days out of thirty-one, whether at home or on the road. Today I also do some full-body stretches to start the routine, and I close my daily session with a few minutes of calisthenics. In forty-five minutes each morning, I'm set for living! Simple. It's my way of life.

It's been my observation that most people know how to walk. I would encourage those who have mastered this skill to use it each and every day. And for those who can't walk, the benefits of upper-body exercise are equally great.

The Law of Physical Activity is not negotiable. Face it. It's time to *just do it.*

People who "woke up" their life through exercise are multitudinous. Carolyn Hess, age seventy-something, of Carlisle, Pennsylvania, became increasingly incapacitated by arthritis. Warm-water hydrotherapy exercise changed her life. "Now I can walk, cook, and even shoot a game of pool with my great-grandson. It's the exercise that made the difference."

Don Pritchard moved his family from South Dakota to Arizona in search of an allergy-free climate. "We just changed allergies," said Don. "There's more dust on the desert than pollen up north. The real difference is that now I exercise. I ride my bicycle. And guess what? My allergies hardly ever bother me."

Gladys Britton of Westport, Connecticut, age 102, credits an active lifestyle and a broad range of interests for her many years. "I get down on the floor every day and do stretching exercises. And I walk around our building twice each day when the weather permits."

Clive Inlander was diagnosed with prostate cancer at age seventy-seven. "I opted for good medical care, all right. But I also got busy with my self-care. I started to walk. As I walked my body, I talked to my body, making suggestions to get well. Walking and talking. That's why I'm in great health today."

It's the Law of Physical Activity at work. Its power is amazing. I know you know that exercise is necessary to achieve wellness. There's no debate. So what's standing in our way?

Perceived pain! For some, physical pain. For others, emotional.

Of the thousands of people with whom I have worked over the last decade, I can recall only two who said they truly enjoyed their exercise program right from the start. But once people found the right routine and kept at it for a period of weeks, exercise became more than a requirement. It became a pleasure, something they looked forward to every day. It was a joy!

That's it! The Law of Physical Activity linked with the Law of Esprit.

The costs of violating the Law of Physical Activity are too great. You and I simply can't afford to neglect it. It's not hard to develop a "Yes, I can" attitude. Slow and steady is the key. Seek moderate and regular lifelong exercise that is fun, and chances are you'll stick to it.

It's all part of living out the non-negotiable Law of Physical Activity.

5

The Law of
Nutritional Frugality

A little with quiet is the only diet.

—*Scottish proverb*

Luigi Cornaro, a fifteenth-century nobleman from Venice, Italy, is famed in the study of wellness because of a vow he made.

After living a youth filled with overindulgence of every kind, Cornaro resolved that he would mend his ways, pursue moderation in all things, and try to survive until he reached the age of at least one hundred.

His success was outstanding. The average life expectancy of fifteenth-century Italians was about thirty-five years. Luigi lived to be 103! Moreover, he remained active, clear thinking, and creative, recording his life experiences in detail right to the end.

The cornerstone of Luigi Cornaro's success? A spare diet of fruits and vegetables. Cornaro lived on the equivalent of about fifteen hundred calories per day from the age of thirty-seven onward. This honored the ancient Greek and Roman belief in a frugal diet as the secret of longevity.

One fifteenth-century experience does not make for scientific proof or twenty-first-century health policy. But frugal eating is the one activity that has caught the attention of virtually every person who has seriously tried to pursue the wellness journey.

As soon as we mention the word *diet,* two predictable objections always arise. The first has to do with lack of willpower: "I've tried a hundred diets and can't stay on one of them." The mental programming is that we'll fail on any future attempt.

The second predictable objection is taste: "I just love a meal of beef roast and apple dumplings! I'm never going to settle for some tasteless diet, no matter how good it is for me."

Listen carefully: our past behavior does not automatically predict our future behavior. We're not talking about sticking to some rigid diet. We're suggesting a whole new way of life, a new outlook, a changed way of viewing ourselves. And taste? There's absolutely no reason that nutritious can't be delicious.

The core message of the Law of Nutritional Frugality is simple: eat a variety of unprocessed foods, in moderate amounts, during at least three meals, including breakfast, combined with a smart afternoon snack, while drinking eight glasses of pure water and taking a broad-spectrum vitamin-and-mineral supplement each day.

That's not difficult. It takes no monumental willpower. Every bite can be delicious. The biggest change is in our thinking. If we change our thinking about eating, we'll change our life. Just a few of the rewards of following the Law of Nutritional Frugality include:

- more energy and less fatigue;
- better weight control;
- a better chance of maintaining proper cholesterol levels;
- a better chance of preventing a variety of diseases;
- increased self-esteem.

I first met Shari, a nurse, at one of my workshops sponsored by a hospital in Atlanta. For Shari, the battle of the bulge had become a war that never ended. She was thirty-two years old and was almost sixty-five pounds over her ideal weight. Although she had tried every fad diet, her weight had risen steadily since her teen years. Each time she'd diet, Shari would take off fifteen to twenty pounds, and then gain it back, and more, over the next six months.

I suggested that Shari start her wellness program with an affirmation. (This brought into the equation the non-negotiable Law of Mindfulness, which I'll discuss in a later chapter.) She chose the phrase "I am vibrant, happy, and fully alive." I also suggested she start to eat breakfast each day and view any hunger pains as signs of progress.

This approach struck a positive chord with Shari. The affirmation helped lift her depression and reminded her of all the great things she had in her life. She had been skipping breakfast as a calorie-saving strategy, and she found that a small meal at the start of the day sharply reduced her craving for sugary afternoon snacks.

The results, so far, have been spectacular. After four months, Shari lost sixteen pounds "without dieting." She was more energetic than she had been in her teen years. At eight months, she was down a total of twenty-nine pounds and found no difficulty in keeping her weight off. She now participates in a regular aerobics class. "The trimmer me is just somehow gradually taking over," Shari said with a smile.

It's true. If we change our thinking about eating, we will change our lives. The choice is ours.

Assuming our physician has not prescribed a special diet, the Law of Nutritional Frugality provides us with these specific eat-smart guidelines:

- Eat a plant! Fresh fruit and fresh vegetables are now our foods of choice.
- Eat breads and pastas that are made from whole grains.
- Look to grains and legumes for protein. Try brown rice with any type of bean.
- Strictly limit chicken and turkey. Eliminate red meats. ("Flesh" foods are difficult to digest fully and have been linked by some researchers to a variety of illnesses.) If you must have animal protein, try water-packed tuna and steamed or broiled fish.

- Use low-fat or nonfat dairy products. Even some cheeses and ice creams are now made with low-fat or nonfat milk.
- Use monosaturated cooking fats like canola and olive oils. If you have to fry, use a nonstick spray.
- Use fat- and sugar-reduced products. Limit your consumption of foods that contain fat and sugar substitutes.
- Consume caffeine and alcoholic beverages, and salt-cured, pickled, and smoked foods only in moderation.
- Drink eight eight-ounce glasses of pure water each day.
- Keep your total daily calories under the two-thousand mark.
- Take a daily vitamin-and-mineral supplement.

The Law of Nutritional Frugality sounds familiar, doesn't it? The trick is to actually eat this way and enjoy it. Remember the Law of Esprit. If it can't be done with joy, we've missed wellness.

Enjoying this approach to diet and nutrition is not a problem; it's a decision. When I was recovering from cancer, I developed a nutritional program very similar to the one I've described here. As critical as the quality of the food was, my attitude toward the program was more important. I was determined that I would enjoy this way of eating.

Changing our diet is something we choose to do, not something we are forced to do. Instead of dreading it, try saying, "Here's another thing I get to do to help myself! Great!"

Diet is a point of power in my life, something under my direct influence and control. Unlike chemotherapy and radiation, it is something that wasn't done to me; it is something done by me. Wow! Empowerment! I love it!

The Law of Nutritional Frugality helps us focus on an important reality. Our bodies simply do not need and cannot use the typical American daily diet of three thousand–plus calories and eighty grams of fat. Keep on that program and you'll find yourself gaining at least two to five pounds per year. Multiply that over ten or twenty years and you'll understand why you're twenty pounds heavier than you'd like to be. Keep violating this non-negotiable law, and your quality of health and life will suffer.

With eating, less really does mean more. It's the Law of Nutritional Frugality.

6

The Law of
Minimal Medical
Invasiveness

The art of medicine is generally
a question of time.

—Ovid

If violating any of the laws of wellness were a punishable offense, a large portion of Americans would be in jail. By far the most violated law in this book is the Law of Minimal Medical Invasiveness.

Honor and esteem the doctor who says, "We want to treat you right but do only what is absolutely necessary, and with minimum side effects. We're going to help your body heal!" Here is a person who understands the Law of Minimal Medical Invasiveness.

Everybody has an explanation for why health care costs so much, in terms of both time and money. Greedy doctors, inefficient hospitals, patients eager to sue for malpractice, unnecessary tests, risk-averse insurers, mountains of paperwork, excessive care for the elderly and the terminally ill. Take your pick.

The bill is huge. Health care costs us a trillion—yes, trillion!—dollars per year.

As I write this, a huge debate rages in Washington between the president and Congress over health-care reform. But health *care* is really a misnomer. The debate is actually about the way health care is financed. What they're talking about is who's gonna pay, and how much.

The real health-care revolution is right here in these pages! The very concept of total wellness is a revolution. What we should, and must, debate is the efficacy of medicine—the value we get for our health-care dollar.

Who is the most important person on your medical team? Do you think it's your surgeon? Your internist? Your cardiologist or oncologist? Maybe your nurse, a technician, or your spouse?

Understand this clearly: the most important person on your wellness team is you. It is *your* wellness we are talking about. Your health is at stake. You are the central character. You are in charge.

One of your most important challenges is to ensure that your medical treatment is as minimally invasive as possible while still being appropriate. The facts are startling. Studies show that if you live near a major medical center, for instance, you are more likely to have a prostate operation, a hysterectomy, or any number of other procedures. We have been conditioned to believe that this is good—that quick access to medical care is critical, that these operations are appropriate.

However, the statistics tell us that people who live in rural areas far away from major medical centers and who do not undergo these operations have about the same survival rate as those patients who do have the procedures.

The Law of Minimal Medical Invasiveness does not mean we don't visit a doctor. It does mean we challenge each and every test and procedure. Too often people surrender leadership to their medical team without knowledge of either the prescribed procedures or the expected outcome.

One of the saddest and most suppressed statistics of our time is that the rate of hospital-acquired infections has doubled over the last ten years. According to the People's Medical Society, 35 to 40 percent of all hospital patients come to the hospital because of something a doctor did to them. *Four of every ten people admitted to the hospital are there as a result of the medical care they received.* And if you add up all the deaths in this country that are estimated to have been the result of medical mishaps, errors, and negligence, you come to a shocking realization: health care is America's third or fourth leading killer!

The Law of Minimal Medical Invasiveness demands that medical *patients* become medical *consumers* and assume a new, proactive role in the treatment of illness and the maintenance of health.

This is especially important for women. The American medical establishment seems to consider being a woman a disease rather than a gender description. Countless medical tragedies have been perpetrated on women. Consider the following:

- the DES and thalidomide fiascos;
- silicone breast implants;

- a 600 percent increase since 1970 in the number of cesarean sections performed;
- estimates that over half of all hysterectomies are unnecessary;
- the common belief that the symptoms of menopause are an illness.

We can't afford to be passive consumers. We must become active participants in our care. What we need is *clinical reform*—the reevaluation of all medical procedures based on medical need and effectiveness rather than financial grounds. And minimal invasiveness lies at the heart of clinical reform.

I ENCOURAGE YOU to see yourself as the manager of a baseball team (or use whatever organizational analogy you like). Your goal is to keep yourself well, or get well again if you are ill. You'll want a strong starting pitcher; many times that is a doctor. And you'll want to assemble other team members: a catcher, infielders, outfielders; equate these with specialists, technicians, family, friends, and a support group, all part of your wellness team. In some cases you may even want a short-term relief pitcher, a surgeon.

But remember who is the manager. You are! You are in charge. You decide who is on the field at any given time.

Knowledge is required to make these decisions. To acquire the facts, we need to *study*. That's right, study!

Become an expert. That's what a real manager does. It's all part of being certain you are receiving the right care.

Know this: the dangers of being overtreated are at least as great as the dangers of being undertreated.

Let's take the case of Al Marconni, for example. Overweight and suffering severe chest pains, he was pushed into bypass surgery. For several months he felt better. But the weight never came off. He still smoked, had a few Scotch and sodas every evening, and seldom exercised. He's now battling emphysema.

What did Mr. Marconni *really* need? It's clear that heart bypass surgery was way down on the list. He needed to change his lifestyle; diet and exercise would have been a good start. And he needed to throw those cigarettes out the window.

But Al Marconni was looking for the easy way to better health. So he agreed to an operation.

Least invasive—that's the seminal issue. How can my health be enhanced with the least physically invasive, the least chemically toxic, the least psychologically violent approach?

Vicki Hufnagel, an obstetrician-gynecologist and gynecologic surgeon, reports in her excellent book *No More Hysterectomies* that hysterectomies are performed in the United States at double the rate for the United Kingdom. "Are we sicker than our Continental cousins?" she asks.

Hufnagel cites the ease and availability of hysterectomies in the United States as the reason for the different rates. She believes the American medical profession must radically change its thinking on elective hysterectomy for benign disease. And patients must become informed, participating in each medical decision. Only then will we be less likely to undergo unnecessary surgery.

The best way to improve health is to change our behaviors. The call goes out for each of us to become better, more informed purchasers of health care. Then we can team up with those who provide health care and demand and get the best, least invasive treatment possible.

Enlightened medical professionals are becoming more numerous. "I learned a lesson twenty-five years ago," said Michigan dentist Robert Ludwig. "The patient in the chair had severe gum tissue disease. I recommended a visit to the periodontist where the diseased tissue would be cut away. The patient said, 'Let me try something for six months. If it doesn't work, then I'll go through with the surgery.'"

Six months later the patient came back with beautiful, healthy gums. "What did you do?" asked an amazed Dr. Ludwig. "Vitamin E," beamed the patient. "Every morning and every evening, I'd bite into a vitamin E gel cap and rub the oil into my gums."

"I was reluctant to share this with my peers," said Dr. Ludwig. "The dental literature reported nothing of this approach and the accepted practice said, 'operate.' But I now believe this has merit in many, many cases."

Least invasive but still appropriate. That's the answer. But when you're a hammer, the whole world looks like a nail; to a hammer, every problem needs a heavy hammer blow. If you're a surgeon, every problem has a surgical cure. If you're a radiation oncologist, every problem has its solution in radiation. If you're a pharmaceutical manufacturer, every problem has a solution in drug form.

The trouble with this approach is that the whole world is not a nail; a hammer blow is not always required. One size does not fit all.

Understand the implications. The Law of Minimal Medical Invasiveness has a corollary that says, "American medicine is first and foremost a business." This means that the people you are counting on aren't always thinking of you first. They have payrolls to meet, mortgages to pay. Sometimes this means you're overtested, overtreated, and given care that does not honor the Law of Minimal Medical Invasiveness.

Medical consumerism, and a commitment to personally practice total wellness, are necessities if we are to live a full life. The guideline of seeking the least invasive yet still appropriate medical care should be inscribed over the doorway of every medical practitioner's office. Until that time comes, we medical consumers will do well to inscribe it in our minds.

It's the Law of Minimal Medical Invasiveness.

Part Three

The Emotional Laws

7

The Law of
Stress-Hardiness

It's not what happens to you.
It's what you do about it.

— *W. Mitchell*
"survivor"

Some people are born lucky. Their genetic makeup programs them for health. Yet many people with all the genetic potential for illness also stay well. That's a mystery worth looking at.

A study compared identical twins with respect to the onset of serious illness. The researchers were puzzled by the marked disparity in the incidence of hereditary diseases: same genetic base, but radically different experiences with illness. How could that be explained? After nearly giving up their efforts, the researchers finally traced the disparate experiences, in large part, to differences in the twins' ability to handle stress.

Stress? Yes, stress! Say hello to the non-negotiable Law of Stress-Hardiness.

After years of research, evidence linking stress to a wide variety of medical conditions is mounting. Both the medical community and the public now agree that stress is a major contributor to health problems like heart attacks, high blood pressure, ulcers, and many nervous disorders. Prolonged stress has even been linked to suppression of the immune function.

It is a fundamental principle of holistic health that the majority of physical illnesses result, at least in part, from an overload of emotional, psychological, and spiritual dis-ease. This overload is an accurate definition of toxic stress.

Enter the Law of Stress-Hardiness, and a surprising conclusion.

The law states that stress is to be not only expected but preferred. The law's corollary states that we can and should welcome stress and that we can and should develop a positive, workable approach to stress management.

It is one thing to expect stress. It is quite another to prepare for stress-related events. But how can stress be preferred, even welcomed?

Think of it. The perfect no-stress environment is the grave. True, I'm making some assumptions here rather than working from personal experience! But although the grave looks peaceful from my perspective, I'm not sure it's preferable.

Stress is an integral part of life. It's a signal that we are alive and part of the flow of this grand experience.

The problem isn't stress, it's toxic stress. This is the anxiety-laden kind, the overload. Yet toxic stress gives us important warning signals, feedback on how we are conducting our lives. And so even it has a positive side.

It's true. The physical feedback from toxic stress includes headaches, indigestion, sleep difficulties, neck and back pain, excessive tiredness, and a ringing in the ears.

The behavioral signs include excess smoking, overuse of alcohol, compulsive eating, bossiness, irritability, and a critical attitude toward others.

The emotional signs of toxic stress are equally obvious. Toxic stress can reduce a grown man to tears, show up as nervousness, be experienced as powerlessness, anger, loneliness, or deep unhappiness. Often stress demonstrates itself as an experience of loss from which there is no hope of recovery.

It all adds up to behavior that includes difficulty in making decisions, an inability to think clearly, constant worry, a loss of creativity, a lack of a sense of humor, and a constant feeling of being overwhelmed.

Do any of these warning signs seem familiar? If so, read with your heart and your mind. The Law of Stress-Hardiness has something to say to you.

I have a toxic-stress signal that never fails me. The incision where my lung was removed "talks" to me! When I try to do too much, it hurts. Pain—pure and simple. I've learned to listen and respond. What are your unique signals?

The Law of Stress-Hardiness includes recognizing the stress warning signals but challenges the myth that there is nothing we can do about them. Passive nonresistance is not the answer. There is plenty we can do.

While we can't control all the circumstances in life, we can effectively control our responses to them. Mindfully choosing a proactive response is the essence of practicing the Law of Stress-Hardiness.

There are hundreds of stress-management programs and techniques that claim to have the answer.
Many are good; several are not. The workable ones have
one key ingredient in common: change.

The Law of Stress-Hardiness requires you to change
two fundamental perceptions: (1) change the perception
of the problem and (2) change the perception of yourself.

The Law of Stress-Hardiness is just that basic. Effectiveness comes in simple packages.

Consider the changes. First, your perception of
the problem: if you perceive the problem as being less
threatening, you remove the toxicity of the stress. Next,
consider the perception of yourself: if you perceive your
ability to handle the problem as significant, the stressors
then become less intimidating.

Arguably, you could manage your toxic stress by
just one change in perception. But increasing personal
power and decreasing problem power is the essence of
stress-hardiness. That's the simple truth of this law.

The Law of Stress-Hardiness implies that we develop a certain active curiosity about stressful events or
circumstances. Through that curiosity and involvement,
we come to a belief that we can influence the event. We
put that personal power into action and recognize that
these challenges are not so much a threat as an opportunity for personal growth on all levels—physical, emotional, and spiritual.

The result: a stress-hardy stance toward life.

The University of Chicago psychologist Suzanne Kobasa has identified the following as stress-hardy characteristics: *control, challenge,* and *commitment.* That's exactly what is involved in changing our perception of the problem and our ability to respond to it. When we change our perception we gain control. The stress becomes a challenge, not a threat. When we commit to action, to actually doing something rather than feeling trapped by the events, the stress in our life becomes manageable.

It's the Law of Stress-Hardiness.

When you look at any of the thousands of stress-management books and articles or see a segment about stress management on your favorite talk show, cut through the fluff and the new techniques. Ask the important questions:

- Does this instruction help me alter my perception of the problem?
- Does this instruction help me improve my ability to respond?

When your answer is yes to both, try it. You can be sure the Law of Stress-Hardiness is at work.

THE MOST COMMON RESPONSE to life-threatening illness is fear. Fear grips. It immobilizes. Life is out of control. Patients see no way to turn. Assumptions about imminent demise quickly follow.

A sense of control is perhaps the most important attribute in the stress-hardy personality. It's the one attribute to cultivate. But we're talking control not over the circumstances, but over our response. Understand that difference! It's true in illness, in relationships, on the job, in all of life! Control our response and we control our life.

"When I demanded a second opinion," shared fifteen-year breast-cancer survivor Colleen Moore, "I realized for the first time I didn't have to turn over control to someone I didn't know, let alone trust. That simple decision was the first in a whole new way of life for me. I learned I could respond. It may be the single most important reason I am alive today."

Change your perception of the problem. Change your perception of your ability to respond.

Michael Benson was a struggling student when he took a stress-management class that taught him to go with the flow. "For ten years I used the nonresistance technique: when faced with a problem, I'd quit. I'd just accept it. Maybe that's why I had a lousy job, no real friends, and was diagnosed as borderline manic-depressive. I was a first-class victim. Thank God, I opened my eyes and realized if I couldn't control the events in my life, I could at least control my response."

Nice going, Michael. We may not be born lucky, but we can choose to make our own luck. That's what the non-negotiable Law of Stress-Hardiness is all about.

8

The Law of
Emotional Choice

Learning to be aware of feelings . . .
is an essential lifetime skill.

—*Joan Borysenko*
author of *Minding the Body, Mending the Mind*

All wellness laws are not created equal.

There's a hierarchy in our lives that governs our sense of satisfaction. The Law of Emotional Choice is near the top of the heap.

Emotional choice. We're talking about our feelings.

Fear, anger, and guilt.

Happiness, contentment, and love.

They're all part of the human experience. You can't expect to prevent the negative feelings altogether. And you can't expect to experience positive feelings all the time. Sometimes negative feelings are absolutely appropriate. The death of a loved one, for example, causes us to feel deeply sad. We need a period of mourning. Or perhaps we've been mistreated and someone is taking advantage of us. Anger follows. These responses are understandable, natural, and healthy.

The Law of Emotional Choice directs us to acknowledge our feelings but also to refuse to get stuck in the negative ones.

The Law of Emotional Choice reminds us not to let unexamined emotions become a "filter" that lets in only those experiences that confirm or reinforce our mood. We have the power of choice! This law encourages us to experience the full range of our emotions.

The Law of Unity introduced us to the concept that body, mind, and spirit work together. The concept of total wellness recognizes that our every thought, word, and behavior affects our greater health and well-being. And we, in turn, are affected not only emotionally but also physically and spiritually.

What? you ask. We are controlled by our emotions at the same time that our emotions are under our control? Precisely. This is a two-way street. It all works together.

Let's fully understand the power of this law. Suppose I told you, "You know, you're a great person. I really like you." How would you feel? And how could you change what you feel?

Some people would be annoyed and suspicious: "Greg's trying to flatter me. He must be trying to get something from me." As we walk away, you feel anger. Other people may feel sad or guilty: "Forget it. Greg is just saying that to make me feel good. He doesn't mean it." And you leave our encounter a bit more depressed. If you're feeling good about the compliment, you're probably thinking, "Gee, Greg likes me. That's great." And you walk away a bit taller. In each example, the compliment, the external event, was the same. The difference was entirely due to the way you, the recipient, felt about it.

As far as changing what you feel, there's the ever-present two-way emotional street. If, for example, we chose to make just one change in the way we accept a compliment, we could shift not only our emotional out-look but also our physiological and spiritual bearings. The Law of Emotional Choice is that powerful.

I don't want to overlook those people who suffer from dementia and require treatment with medication; the Law of Minimal Medical Invasiveness is an impor-tant one, too. But let's recognize there are cognitive strategies that can be put to use to alter moods and feel-ings. In fact, most people under medication do better when they also contribute to their own well-being by choosing to change.

Jane, a participant in our Total Wellness Program at an assisted living retirement community, was showing signs of early dementia. She complained of both depres-sion and anxiety and came to us already taking the drug Xanax. Physically unable to climb stairs and cook for herself, Jane had recently given up her home. After the move, she became deeply depressed and overwhelmed by the changes in her life. She spent many hours each day sitting around and showed no interest in activities or visitors. She napped during the day but then couldn't sleep at night. She wouldn't exercise and asked for a walker.

Jane agreed to enter the program. She committed herself to a program of daily exercise—in itself a major benefit since it broke the pattern of her inertia. She started to socialize, talking to others, learning that they, too, were afraid.

The more Jane reached out to others in the program, the less anxious and depressed she felt. Her appetite increased, and she gained a much-needed ten pounds. Today Jane has a greatly increased ability to cope with life and looks forward to the future with a new sense of enthusiasm. She chose wellness.

The Law of Emotional Choice often flies in the face of traditional counseling and psychotherapy in that it says that knowing the origins of our negative patterns or early emotional conditioning is *not* essential to changing the way we feel about ourselves!

Take, for example, depression—the common cold of emotional problems. It encompasses a number of feelings including loss, defeat, discouragement, lack of energy, and hopelessness. Depressed people feel pessimistic. They view their future as bleak and themselves as worthless and inadequate.

The traditional, purely psychological approach would be to focus on how our past has made our present. But what if we simply decided to do something to change our mood? Those who look within, who sincerely ask themselves why they feel down and what they can do to change their mood—for example, can they attempt to view the situation differently, exercise, go for a walk in the sun, begin a new project, or extend themselves in the service of another person? — will do wonders in overcoming depression.

"I spent eight years in therapy," said Gloria, a nursing-home administrator. "The only thing that improved was my therapist's bank account. It was awful. I quit when she insisted my low self-esteem was related to childhood abuse by my father. I decided I wouldn't focus on the past. Instead, I started to exercise every day. I believe exercise, more than anything else, changed my emotional outlook. In a real sense, I chose my emotions."

Look at the progression. Different behavior leads to different thoughts, which leads to different results. Body influences mind, which influences spirit. Any proposed boundary between these elements is open to debate. They all work as one. They are all under our control.

It's the Law of Emotional Choice. We can choose to become proactive.

Though so far I've talked mostly about depression, the law applies equally to some of the other, more powerful toxic emotions. Think about it: anger and hostility are literally killers. Anger is the intense but fleeting emotion directed at someone or something. Look at the newspaper: anger leads to violence every day. Hostility is the more global result of hanging on to one's anger. Hostility has been described as anger turned into resentment. It shows up as opposition, resistance, and antagonism. It's a very difficult way to live and contrary to all the laws of wellness.

Chronic hostility springs from the mind. Constant boil-overs boil down to a deep-seated cynical mistrust of others. The supermarket checker—you automatically reason without a shred of evidence—was *of course* trying to rip you off when he rang up that can of orange juice twice. And that darned pedestrian taking forever to cross the street in front of your car—she just wants to make you wait. And you know why a co-worker got that plum assignment instead of you—*the boss is out to get you!* It all adds up to hostile resentment.

The Law of Emotional Choice does not imply that we'll never know anger or hostility, nor does it suggest that we always have to be calm and take everything quietly. In fact, anger can be used purposefully: anger is energy that mobilizes us to change otherwise destructive situations.

But chronic hostility, often coupled with a fault-finding, basic mistrust of people, is an issue under our control. As with depression, when a person will sincerely attempt to use the Law of Emotional Choice in coping with hostility, help is near.

When we stop to ask ourselves questions like "Why am I so angry?" "Is my reaction really helpful?" "Is this the way I want to spend my time?" we shape a constructive response.

The heart of the Law of Emotional Choice is to take personal responsibility for our moods. Simple things, like taking a walk or renting a funny movie, are, for the vast majority of people, not manifestations of classic denial. Rather, they are the very stuff that changes moods. Of course, if we have been depressed or rabid with anger for several weeks, and all efforts to overcome this mood have failed, it is then wise to seek professional counsel.

But the Law of Emotional Choice challenges us to ask ourselves if it is realistic to respond to the situation differently. Instead of sitting in our darkened room, maybe it's time to get out and walk in the fresh air. Instead of focusing on what goes into and comes out of our bodies, maybe it's time to extend ourselves, to help someone else. Instead of holding on to a burning coal of resentment, maybe it's time to forgive. In the simplest terms, instead of giving in to our lack of energy or the desire to do nothing or the urge to seek revenge, maybe it's time to do something different.

Even chronic fear and crippling anxiety can be positively influenced by the Law of Emotional Choice. Healthy fears alert us to danger and keep us safe from troubles. But constant anxiety comes from grossly distorted thoughts that have little or no basis in reality. Those thoughts can paralyze us.

Again, long-term psychoanalysis is probably not required. Fears that paralyze amount to false evidence appearing real. We "awfulize," if you will, imagining outcomes at their worst. We avoid confronting our fears. The more we avoid fear, the more it captures our entire being.

The best way to confront fears and anxieties is to invoke the Law of Emotional Choice. Face the fear. Do something about it. Push through it. Go for it! "When I walked off that airplane," said Tiffany, a nineteen-year-old college freshman who was paralyzed at the idea of flying, "it was as if I'd won a gold medal. I did it!"

The person who will face the fear or anxiety and act, even in some small, positive way, is exercising the Law of Emotional Choice. This is wellness at its finest. For not only will the choice likely dissipate the fear, it will also build the needed self-confidence that will unlock many more of the gifts of life.

Consistently exercising the Law of Emotional Choice builds an inner strength that is unshakable. This is self-esteem of the best and highest order. Now we accurately measure ourselves and our limitless potential. We come to a recognition that we are divinely inspired and have wondrous abilities. A new spirit suffuses our very being. A brighter self-image influences our moods, our behavior, and ultimately our entire life. Our heart can smile again.

If all the laws of wellness were ranked by popularity, few would receive more votes. The winner? The non-negotiable Law of Emotional Choice.

9

The Law of
Developmental
Motivation

Use what talents you possess:
the woods would be very silent
if no birds sang except
those that sang best.

— *Henry Van Dyke*

There exists a profound truth in the understanding of human behavior: only unsatisfied needs motivate!

There also exist two types of motivation: developmental motivation and deficiency motivation. Both fulfill unsatisfied needs. However, one leads to a satisfying life; the other, to a life of discontent. Understanding and practicing developmental motivation is crucial to experiencing wellness.

For years I struggled with trying to motivate myself. I used all the psyche-up techniques. The benefits were temporary, at best.

Then came a revelation. I had been attempting to motivate myself from the standpoint of what was wrong with me. Dr. Wayne Dyer, with unparalleled insight, calls this approach "deficiency motivation." It's a no-win way to live life.

I would assess all the things I was missing: love, money, possessions. I thought I was missing it all. I viewed my life as eternally deficient. On and on grew the list of what was missing.

I'd think, "When I get a new car, then I'll be happy"; "As soon as I find the right life partner, that's when my life will be complete." Following all the mind-numbing, soul-draining techniques on the self-help shelf, I would set a goal, create a burning desire, think positive, and drive myself crazy!

It was a huge trap. When we motivate ourselves from this mind-set, we can never know life satisfaction. Why? Because we'll always suffer from the dreadful disease called "more."

I'd get the new car. But in less than a week I would be dissatisfied. Somebody else had a better one. I'd travel the world, but in a couple of months I'd grouse about having to live out of a suitcase. Other lifestyles always seemed to offer more.

What was wrong was my motivating mind-set. I was motivating myself from what was missing in my life. I may have satisfied a want, but my mind-set was never satisfied. I was always focused on wanting more—on striving, not arriving.

Deficiency motivation is a practice that is repeated across international boundaries. From Europe and Africa to the Middle East and Asia, the thought "I don't have enough" is widely held. In the world of personal motivation, if you focus on the something that is missing, guess what? The perceived lack will expand. Something will always be missing. What's deficient in your life will become your calling card, your life experience.

Enter the great non-negotiable Law of Developmental Motivation.

The essence of the law is this: I am complete but not finished. This is a statement of powerful truth.

You are complete, whole, and fully alive right now! You need no more for life to be happy. You can be completely fulfilled with what is, now.

Of course we're not yet finished. Even though we are complete, growth, change, and becoming are part of life. Our physical body constantly replaces itself with new cells. Our mental capacities grow. Our spiritual reality provides a constant source of renewal. We grow and change naturally—by choice, not from lack.

We are complete now, yet our natural development calls for further growth. This shift in thinking is critical. Lacks become impossible. When we can see the inevitability of growth and change, we begin to become motivated by our dreams, not our deficiencies.

We feel fully alive because lack is no longer part of our thinking process. We no longer see ourselves as deficient. We are free to grow and change—but not because we are incomplete. Instead, we seek growth and change because we are internally motivated to give, to serve, and to love.

This is the Law of Developmental Motivation. It changes the way we perceive achievement and view life.

Walt Kallestad is the pastor of the Community Church of Joy in Glendale, Arizona. He makes this point well. When Walt stopped trying to build the church to satisfy his own ego and started to work solely out of a mind-set of service to others, the church started to grow. No longer operating out of a deficiency mind-set, he was free to grow out of a deep commitment to love and serve.

Our greatest perceived need is physical survival. The second-greatest perceived human need is psychological survival. The third is spiritual survival. There is a hierarchy of the perceptions: physical, psychological, and spiritual. Body, mind, spirit. In that order.

Satisfied needs, be they physical, psychological, or spiritual, do not motivate. Only unsatisfied hungers move people. This is one of the most powerful understandings we can have of ourselves and of others.

But the mere fact that we have unsatisfied needs does not mean we are deficient.

No. With the Law of Developmental Motivation, we're seeking the complete development of our life potential. That's total wellness. And for the practice of total wellness to become an experienced reality, three key elements must come together: *knowledge, skill,* and *desire*.

Study these elements. Knowledge is the "what to do" and the "why to do it"; each of the non-negotiable laws represents what must be done to accomplish a higher level of wellness. Skill is the "how to do it"; a daily process, a way of thinking, a disciplined response to life—all are part of the skills category. Desire is the motivation, the "want to do it" that is needed to bring knowledge and skill into reality. If we are missing just one of those three elements we won't have wellness.

Knowledge and skill are the simple parts. It's desire that stands in the way of most seekers of wellness.

During the last decade, I have counseled thousands

of people going through all types of illness. Many will say they'll do anything to get well again. They just want their health back.

A woman wrote to me proclaiming, "I'll do absolutely anything to get well. Where do I start?"

That's deficiency motivation. And it has been my observation that most people who are motivated in this way don't do too well. They're trying to not die, to overcome the "deficiency" of lost health.

"I just want things back to normal," wrote another patient. "If only my life were like it was two years ago." But hey, "normal" is what contributed to the problem in the first place! We don't want to be motivated by our lacks. We need a vision of what might be.

In my observations, the people who have the most success are those who, in spite of illness, do all they can to live for today. These are the ones who see life as complete even though it may have some health challenges. They have made an essentially spiritual decision to live now.

This stands in contrast to society's uncomfortable defensiveness about the process of dying. Most people do everything possible to ignore death, particularly any thoughts of their own demise, and will go to extremes to avoid an anxiety-laden discussion about it.

At one of our weeklong retreats, a woman named Patty, who was dealing with recurrent breast cancer, shared her experience. "In my family, it's absolutely taboo to talk about death. My husband walks out of the room. He's frightened. Same thing with my parents. But what about my fears? It's not at all helpful."

That week we helped her challenge the family's collective denial. Patty finally came to the realization that death was part of life's bargain. She wrote in her course evaluation, "The most important thing I learned was to stop dying of cancer and start living with cancer. I've resolved to master death by living life."

"The turning point in my health," wrote Bessie, a very active resident of a retirement community, "was when I decided to forget my troubles and live to be 100!" Will she make it? I don't know. But her new motivation is infinitely superior to the motivation of those who want to fill a deficiency in their lives.

It's not that we don't want to make and keep commitments to ourselves. It's that our motivation to correct a deficiency is wrong. It can't carry us for long. What we really need is a new vision.

When we are motivated by goals that have deep meaning, by dreams that need completion, by pure love that needs expressing, then we truly live life! For many, this often means a longer life.

The type of motivation that drives our lives is an important part of experiencing total wellness. A deep sense of fulfillment comes only from a serious commitment to a life filled with purpose, with striving for higher ideals. Therein lies true happiness.

It's the non-negotiable Law of Developmental Motivation.

Part Four

The Social Laws

10

The Law of
Human Dignity

God created man in his own image.

—*Genesis*

Aretha Franklin's great song "Respect" says it all. Just imagine her singing it now:

"R-E-S-P-E-C-T.
Find out what it means to me."

Those are more than mere words. They're all about one of the most critical wellness commodities in the world today—respect for the individual person.

It's the Law of Human Dignity.

When I say "human dignity" and "respect for the individual person," I'm talking about our specific, day-to-day attitudes and behaviors. It is here that we actually practice respect, person to person, not in some abstract "love of mankind" that we hear about in church or civics class.

This active daily awareness of the dignity of the person, the constant awareness of the worth and value of every person regardless of race, color, age, gender, or economic situation, this awareness of high value and supreme worth is fundamental to individual and social wellness.

I believe every person in this world is a creation of God, and that he or she is worthy of my respect. This is the fundamental concept behind the Law of Human Dignity.

What keeps this great non-negotiable wellness law from becoming a daily reality around this intimate little planet is the fact that we constantly put people in "little boxes." We label and categorize, pushing individuals and even nations into little slots. We become so obsessed with relating to people in those little boxes that we never get around to seeing them as unique individuals of great worth and destiny!

The boxes are everywhere. Religion: "He's a Christian"; "Well, he's Muslim"; "She's Jewish." And we categorize by those labels: "If he's a Christian, he must be one of those anti-abortion protesters who are out shooting doctors"; "Muslim? Those terrorists!"; "She's Jewish? You just know she's driven by money and ego."

Stereotypes are everywhere. We talk about a co-worker according to whether he went to this school or was in that graduate program. Has this degree or that honor. Works at this job or in that location. Drives a Mercedes or a Chevy. Has a home in this neighborhood or rents in that building. Is of Caucasian ancestry or comes from Asia. Speaks with a Spanish accent or in an Indian dialect.

The Law of Human Dignity won't allow for such categorizing and judging. Respect is the key.

I'M A CONSULTANT to a large multicampus health-care organization. The company's mission is to provide assisted retirement living that fills a wide range of needs. This may involve something as simple as providing an apartment with weekly cleaning services or something as complex as arranging twenty-four-hour personal nursing care for an Alzheimer's patient.

The company employs twelve hundred workers in jobs that cover every occupational, educational, social, and economic stratum. And in striving toward a democratic outlook, it tries its best to foster the idea that there are no distinctions between job classifications. But the lines of delineation on some campuses are very strong.

Job titles give it all away. Some jobs are classified as professional, and others are not. Some positions require extensive training, and others simply involve being shown how the dishwasher is unloaded. Those that require more education are better paying. It's that simple.

Frankly, the single most effective person I've met in the organization, at least in terms of meeting residents' needs, is a woman named Jeanne. She does not have a fancy title, an education, the pay, or the prestige. What she does have is everyone's respect. She is admired by the residents, her peers, and most co-workers. Jeanne is constantly positive without being insincere. You receive a lift just by being around her.

Yet when I singled Jeanne out for praise to a group of supervisors, the first comment I heard, from one of the more highly educated supervising nurses, was "She hasn't even graduated from community college." Do you see the little box in which the supervisor had stuffed Jeanne?

Too bad. Things like higher education are viewed with a kind of mania in our society. A person like Jeanne, though obviously skilled in her work, is viewed as "less than" simply because she does not have a college degree. The supervisor might as well have said, "I don't really want to know who you are, what you can do, what the condition of your heart is, what strengths you have, or what obstacles you have overcome. I just want to see your college degree." That's certainly what was embedded in the remark.

The Law of Human Dignity stands for exactly the opposite. The Law says we value individuals: we want to know who they are, what they can do, where their hearts are; we want to know about their life journeys, their hopes and dreams, and the compassion that lies in their souls.

There are many, many little boxes into which we slot people. One that crosses international boundaries is money. Material wealth is the most highly overregarded personal attribute in the world. Having lots of money does not automatically make you a model citizen. Plenty of fools have money. But around the world people without money or a college education are constantly deprived of the chance to show their real worth.

I recently attended a meeting on leadership and customer-service development held by and for the managers of one of America's largest and most prestigious health-care corporations. I sat through this all-day meeting with people who had medical degrees, doctorate degrees, and degrees in health-care administration. Nearly eight hundred attended.

All day long I heard comments that conveyed a deep, though unintentional, disrespect for the "frontline" people of health care. *Frontline* was a reference, as best I could decipher it, to the nurses, the lab technicians, the radiation technologists, the social workers, and the office staff. In short, it was a reference to the people who spend the most time with the patients— the actual customers the organization is trying to serve.

What amazed me was the low esteem in which several of the speakers held the frontline workers. I listened to comments like: "With some training, we can make them better people." One woman actually said, "My goal is to at least get our little nurses to smile."

The administrative director of one of the company's large medical centers got up and said, "I fired a person because she didn't make eye contact when she spoke." He concluded by saying, "She was *just* a receptionist."

I couldn't take it anymore. I happened to be the evening's main speaker. I changed my entire talk. In my opening remarks I said, "Ladies and Gentlemen, with all humility, and fully aware of my status as an outside guest who has no economic stake in this organization, I need to say something of singular importance to you and your task of leadership development in health care.

"Unless and until you develop a deep and sincere respect for the frontline people in your organization, you can forget the task of leadership development.

"Every frontline person in this organization is an immensely worthy human being no matter what position he or she holds, no matter what degree follows his or her name."

I continued, with all the volume and vigor I could muster: "Immediately change your attitude about these people, to recognize and praise their human dignity. Then, and only then, will you show respect and, as a result, will you get the respect that will allow you to lead."

Don't misunderstand me or the Law of Human Dignity. I'm all for college education and very much in favor of people having material prosperity in their lives. I stand for every kind of advancement anyone can make. But if we want to make this world a better place, we cannot draw up some set of artificial criteria based on position, power, education, or wealth and dismiss anyone and everyone who doesn't fit them. And the sad fact is, that's what we're doing. The Law of Human Dignity calls for a massive and wrenching change.

I recognize the value that education can bring. I scratched and clawed my way through college on my own. But if I'm better for anything, it is not for the college education. It is for the life education, the lessons I learned as I worked my way through school. They have served me well.

I'm not one bit better as a person because I have a degree or two. Nor is the woman who cleans my office any less worthy or important because she didn't go beyond the third grade.

The practice of human dignity is in our attitudes and our words. Catch yourself saying "just" (as in "just a mechanic"), and eliminate it! The "professionals" in this world get told every day what a fine job they are doing. But people from all areas of life do their jobs with pride and contribute to the world with great competence. These workers are the framework of our organizations, our country, and the world. Esteem them. Praise them. Treat them with human dignity!

I DID SOME CONSULTING WORK with an organization whose chief operating officer, a bright and degreed professional, shows disdain for anyone who makes a mistake. When I interviewed the people who report to him, the first issue that came up was lack of trust. They feared him.

No wonder the organization can't move ahead. It's floundering because a giant redwood from the forest has fallen across the path—the fallen redwood of a manager violating the Law of Human Dignity.

A person is not a leader until his or her people accept him or her as their leader. She might be a boss, a manager, even a master, but still not a leader. He may gain control over people by various means, even attempt to impose control by making threats, but unless the Law of Human Dignity is at work, leadership is never conferred.

Great leadership is tied to human dignity. We are all required to be leaders, each in a different way. Some in politics, some in business, some in our places of worship, all of us in our homes and families. Without respect for the people we lead, it is impossible for us to be effective leaders.

But with the practice of human dignity, magic happens. When aspiring leaders practice daily respect, lives, organizations, and nations are changed. Followers return respect and affection in equal proportion to the respect and affection they're shown. People know when another person respects them for what they are, and they will follow that kind of leader. This law should be self-evident.

Respect for one's followers does not mean softness or a sacrifice of high standards and goals. It means that a genuine faith exists, a bond and covenant between those leading and those led. If people know that their leader has faith in them, they will usually do whatever is humanly possible to measure up.

THE LAW OF HUMAN DIGNITY carries with it a mandate: to stop our pettiness and quit putting each other in little boxes that diminish the dignity and potential of all. In short, when you give me respect and I give you respect, we will both be better for it.

On such fundamentals turns a better world.

11

The Law of
Win/Win

Do unto others as you
would have others do unto you.

—*The Golden Rule*

Too many people go through life always trying to be winners. "I'm going to win if it's the last thing I do," they say. The relationship toll of this pathway is very, very high.

There is a better way: the Law of Win/Win. This law must be understood within the context of four paradigms of social interaction.

Win/Lose

One model is win/lose: "If I win, you lose." In sports, for instance, only one team or one player wins; the other loses. In relationships we think along the same lines: "If you get your way, I don't get mine." Winning, by definition, creates losers. Or so we think.

Comparisons are at the heart of the win/lose mentality. Two children in the same family are pitted against one another with phrases like "Your sister is a lot smarter than you." Most sales incentive programs are set up so that only the top people "win," even if others also do exceptionally well. These dynamics create win/lose environments that ultimately undermine an organization. By grading on the curve, teachers interpret an individual student's value by comparing him or her to everyone else, not to his or her own ability. With a model like this, we all lose.

What the win/lose model communicates is that a person has value only in comparison with somebody else or against some expectation. But most of life does not operate that way. Most results depend on cooperation, not competition. Win/lose has but limited value in relationships and must be strictly limited to low-trust situations.

Lose/Win

Another model of social interaction is lose/win: "I will lose so that you can win." People who want peace at any price often adopt this attitude. They enter a relationship and are quick to please. They have minimal demands and low expectations.

Lose/win people tend not to express their own feelings and convictions, and they tend to be easily intimidated by others. Hoping to gain power from popularity and acceptance, they typically capitulate, giving in and giving up.

Many people with cancer have a deep streak of lose/win. I see this characteristic more in women than in men. Seeking to appease and rescue, they lay down their health, fulfilling the role model of giver. The cost is high in terms of resentment, despair, and repressed emotions.

Lose/win is not a strong position; it indulges others. But it cannot last for long. Self-sacrifice has limits that show early.

Lose/Lose

Lose/lose is a social model that is highly toxic. Typically lose/lose results when two high-powered win/lose people interact. Egos inflate. Wills rush to the fore. Both people say, "It must be done my way." The result is lose/lose. Both will lose. Both people will want to win at all costs, to the point of blaming the other for any problem and then vowing to inflict some form of payback. Revenge has a high price; the execution of the self.

I recently met with a man who is experiencing metastatic prostate cancer. It's now in his liver; the jaundice is severe. When I was with him he talked incessantly, always the adversary. He talked about the "son of a bitch who tried to back out of a real-estate deal." He said he was going to "get him," that he was "declaring war on that bastard."

Lose/lose is the philosophy of the adversary. Trouble is, at the end of the day everyone is the victim.

Win/Win

Win/win is the state of mind and heart that constantly seeks to find the mutually beneficial position in all human relationships. When we're into win/win, all people involved in a transaction not only support the decision but actually feel good about the plan and are committed to implementing it.

Win/win is a paradigm of cooperation, not competition; of allies, not adversaries. Win/win assumes that one's person's success will not be achieved at the expense of another.

The Law of Win/Win says, "Let's not do it your way or my way; let's do it the best way."

IN WIN/LOSE SITUATIONS I may get my way on a particular issue with you, but your attitudes toward me and your trust in our relationship have been damaged. My short-term win turns into a long-term loss. In lose/win situations, we have the reverse. You may get what you want for the moment, but my attitude toward you will change. A focus on your win without any consideration of my needs has no future. Lose/lose is not viable in any context. It's an Adolf Hitler approach to life that means everybody loses everything.

Let's face it. In most of life we really are interdependent. We need each other. Staunch independence is an illusion, but heavy dependence isn't healthy, either. The only position of long-term strength is interdependence: win/win.

I was recently invited to conduct a stress-management seminar for a group of salespeople at a division of a large pharmaceutical company. What I didn't realize initially, the senior vice president of marketing soon made clear. He had recently had to tell his sales reps that their commissions were being cut. They saw the change as lose/win, with management—of course—coming out on top.

During an initial question-and-answer period, what began as a discussion of stress management quickly turned into a conflict-resolution workshop. The salespeople were furious, feeling deeply hurt and betrayed. We needed to come up with a win/win solution or mass revolt seemed likely.

It's difficult for a person or a company to admit to being wrong. And it's often unrealistic to expect such an admission. Framing issues in win/win terms is often the only real way to resolve conflict.

In the past, the management of this organization went out of its way to be generous in every way. Now, economics were forcing cost controls. The company was in real jeopardy.

In being honest, in telling the salespeople that the change in the commission structure was necessary to help bolster the stock price, management was able to create a deeper understanding. Now the salespeople could begin to see how the company's health was in their best interest as well. A win/win situation.

I still work with this sales force. Progress has been made. We are now at the point of compromise, a lower form of win/win. Most important, the win/win mentality has started to permeate the organization, replacing win/lose scripts that had been in place for twenty years.

What's different? The non-negotiable Law of Win/Win. As fundamental as this law is to human relationships, it is constantly violated. And the cost is high.

In order for win/win to work, it must be founded on strong personal character. In a word, we're looking for *trust*. Trust is the essence of win/win. When present, it creates an atmosphere of open communication, a synergy of real creativity.

There are no shortcuts on the path of total wellness. Like it or not, personal social satisfaction comes only after the work of personal character development.

We're talking about our personal involvement in relationships and in group settings—the very stuff most of life seems to be made of.

Sometimes it seems that all of life is a relationship. We have relationships with everything—from people to food to possessions, even to this book, and especially with ourselves.

The relationships we have with the world are largely determined by the relationships we have with ourselves. And that relationship is highly influenced by the relationships we had as children with the adults around us. Our childhood experiences still color our behavior today. Either we mirror the way adults reacted to us, or we react against it.

The only way we'll change our relationships is to change ourselves. Whether our troubles are with a friend, lover, spouse, child, relative, boss, co-worker, or employee, when we see something we don't like in another, what we see is a direct reflection of ourselves. It's a look in the mirror. When we change our own patterns of relating, we find that the friend, spouse, child, or boss changes too.

The trouble comes when we start to lay blame. When we blame, we give away our power. When a child (or adult) says, "You make me mad," the implicit assumption is "I'm mad but you have to change." What happened to the control? For this situation to resolve itself, someone *else* has to change. The person with the problem has just rendered herself or himself powerless.

Let's not give our considerable power away. Without power, we can never take responsibility for making the changes that improve our lives. Give away power and we become helpless victims.

There is a better way. It's the Law of Win/Win.

A vibrant marriage is impossible without win/win as its centerpiece. Parenting is a nightmare without deep unconditional love and respect coupled with a win/win attitude. Friendships, school and community activities, philanthropy—all live or die around the Law of Win/Win.

But what if you commit yourself to the Law of Win/Win and your commitment is not reciprocated? Perhaps others haven't even heard of win/win, or maybe they are deeply scripted in win/lose.

It's now time for a test. Win/win isn't always the easiest achievement, especially in the short term. But if one, just one person in the relationship will make the statement and keep the position that he or she will seek a mutually beneficial solution, we will always come out better than if we had kept silent.

We must stay longer in the communication process. We must express ourselves with greater courage. At the same time, we must listen more carefully and in greater depth. Win/win means we strive for understanding first. We seek to be understood second.

The essence of wellness in difficult relationships is to become an example for the other person. Keep communication lines open until the other person begins to realize that you genuinely want to resolve the issue in a way that is truly win/win for both. When we do this, we succeed in ways we never before imagined.

The Law of Win/Win hinges on this process. First understand, then be understood, and strive for mutual benefit. The more committed we are to genuinely, sincerely giving ourselves to the mutually beneficial outcome, the more powerful our influence on the other person will be. Win/win goes beyond finding a "solution" and toward committing all parties to a higher way. Now we can see that each of us will get more of what he or she wants by going for what it is that we both want.

That's transformation! That's a new, "weller" life. That's the non-negotiable Law of Win/Win.

12

The Law of
Present-Moment
Living

Be here now.

—*Ram Dass*

My twelve-year-old daughter teaches me more than I teach her. One of the best lessons she demonstrates is how to use time. She has a thousand activities: art, dance, tennis, swimming, reading, crafts. She jumps from one to another with enthusiasm.

She never wants to go to bed, fearing she might miss another opportunity to explore, learn, and have fun. Yet, when she does go to bed, she falls asleep almost immediately. Then it's up in the morning and more excitement. She's filled with a zest for living, an alive curiosity, a joy for life.

My daughter's philosophy of time is similar to one that I saw printed on a bumper sticker outside a Weight Watchers® meeting: "Life is short. Eat dessert first!" She relates almost exclusively to the immediate present, to right now. I suspect she considers the world her toy box, and she is not about to leave any toy unexplored.

Some people would criticize the approach my wife and I have taken in raising this child. Beyond a basic set of values, we have attempted to instill the idea that life is filled with unlimited potential. We have repeatedly encouraged our daughter to tap that potential not in the past, not in the future, but in the now!

Most of us who are adults tend to accept the idea that time cannot be spent solely in the moment. We emphasize past lessons and project them into the future. We often take on the attitude of "That's the way things have been done in the past. That's how we'll do them in the future."

It's difficult to challenge our long-standing past-present-future mental tapes. We tend to believe the past will continue to repeat itself in this moment and in future moments no matter what, without the possibility of change. I notice that my daughter very seldom constrains herself by thoughts of the past.

The future can rob us of present-moment possibilities. We can become so obsessed with the future that we pollute the now.

It's the old "what if"—a future-driven endless string of questions that lead to misery. How often we catch ourselves thinking:

> "What if this doesn't work as planned?"
> "What if somebody finds out I'm inadequate?"
> "What if . . . ?"

You know the drill. More about this in a later chapter.

By the time we consider every contingency, there's no time left for the special magic of life available in this moment. I notice that my daughter doesn't seem to have many "what if" problems.

Dragging the past into the present, or living a life based on undefined future "maybes," is a certain ticket to despair. The Law of Present-Moment Living is the only way out.

I spoke about present-moment living to a packed hall in San Diego recently. A woman came up afterward, struggling with a cane, carrying a portable pump through which chemotherapeutic chemicals were being continuously infused into her body. I spotted her as she stood in the long line. She finally made her way to the front. "I have chosen to die," she said. "I don't want to live for the moment, any moment."

Sensing that her words might be only partially true—after all, she *was* attending my talk—I responded, "You still need to live in this moment. If you don't, you'll pollute every minute between now and your death. You might as well enjoy every remaining moment." She left smiling, shaking her head and probably wondering about my optimism.

Yet I could not have given better advice. I've seen dozens of people who, once they have resolved the issue of accepting death and have "given in to the inevitable," release themselves to live life fully. Once we begin to appreciate the present moment, we start to realize what a wonderful place life is, no matter what the circumstances.

The essence of the Law of Present-Moment Living is this: if you're taking part in activities and entertaining thoughts that do not support life, that make you wallow in misery and indulge in negative thinking, then, no matter what you may claim to the contrary, you are polluting the moment.

If you are immersed in life-enhancing activities and enjoying them with positive enthusiasm, then you are living in the moment. This is a dimension of wellness we are never going to know unless and until we cultivate a consciousness of living in the now.

Once I was in Fargo, North Dakota, in the middle of March, doing a seminar. Some will question my judgment in agreeing to do a seminar in Fargo in March. In any case, the morning of the event, I awoke early to do my exercises. The hotel room I was provided with overlooked a large, beautiful atrium complete with lush green plants and a swimming pool. My room had no window to the outside, which meant I hadn't a clue about the day's weather.

I donned my running clothes, pulled out an old stocking cap, and made my way to the exit. I was greeted with wind-whipped snow and temperatures of minus twelve degrees!

Yet I want the record to show I am no fair-weather exerciser. I bravely went out—about ten yards. Back in I came! That day, I did my exercises in the warmth of the enclosed swimming pool!

Perhaps it was all perfectly planned. For there poolside at 6:30 A.M. was a person I would come to know as

Miss Ida. She was from Bismarck and had made the trip in the middle of winter just to be part of the seminar.

She was a little person, charming, nattily dressed in a colorful warm-up. Her gracious personality, her speech with just a hint of an accent, marked her as one of those old-fashioned gentlewomen of years gone by. I spotted her near the Jacuzzi doing her morning stretches. She recognized me and was poolside as I got out.

"Excuse me for bothering you," she apologized as she introduced herself. "My name's Miss Ida." She said that's what everyone had called her since she was married at fifteen. Miss Ida was direct and came quickly to the point, which indicated to me she had sharp mental capacity. She was businesslike.

Her husband had died nearly two years before. She had developed cancer of the colon just six months later. The deterioration of her health was now overwhelming. She missed her husband, which added to her misery.

"We had such a wonderful life together," she recalled. "It was all so pleasant. Then one night, my sweetheart went home to be with God. It was so sudden.

"I have had to reorganize my entire life. But I can't seem to get it done. I just think of him. We always lived well, and it was a shock to discover I had so little money to live on. My husband never discussed business with me. And I don't think I would have grasped it if he had. I found we had debts to pay off. And when it was all settled, I realized I needed to work.

"But, Mr. Anderson, I can't do just anything. I've never had training. I was a housewife and mother. I have no ability and talent. And now I have cancer. I just wish my dear sweetheart would come back. Then everything would be okay again."

It was pretty plain to see that Miss Ida was letting her mind trick her. She was living in the past. I sat down and we talked.

"Commit yourself to life," I encouraged her. "Now, I don't mean commit yourself to living a certain number of years. I mean commit yourself to living each day, fully, productively, joyfully. Commit yourself to wellness, even with cancer—not as a distant dream, but as a here-and-now reality."

I told Miss Ida about not putting off living her life until she was "cured" of cancer. I told Miss Ida not to delay living fully because she was alone, without her husband. I told her not to put her life on hold because she did not have all the money she wanted.

I told her, "Come away today with a commitment to start doing the things you've always wanted to do. Start enjoying each moment by finding something enjoyable in it now!"

WE ALL CARRY a tendency to put life on hold pending the resolution of some problem. We say, "When my life is better, I'll be able to start focusing on positive things." This is a big mistake.

Start now!

The Law of Present-Moment Living is the antithesis of procrastination. We can put off unpleasant activities, but in doing so we also put off the enjoyable ones. We ration our pleasure and contentment as if the supply were limited.

Yet the truth—and it is a great truth—is this: the supply of misery, pain, and suffering is unlimited, but so is the supply of pleasure, contentment, and fulfillment. It is we who do the rationing.

Ration no more! Capture wellness this instant! This instant is all there is. Live it!

It's the great non-negotiable Law of Present-Moment Living.

Part Five

The Intellectual Laws

13

The Law of
Mindfulness

The mind is its own place,
and in itself
can make a heaven of Hell,
a hell of Heaven.

— *John Milton*

Only one thing has to change for us to know happiness in our lives: where we focus our attention. The good news is that we *can* choose.

Welcome to the non-negotiable Law of Mindfulness.

Part of my work takes me into an assisted-living retirement community on a weekly basis. One of the residents, a woman named Florence, has severe arthritis and constantly complains that she can't walk.

But the fact is, she can walk—some days with the help of a cane or a walker, other days on her own. To be sure, she is slower than she was in her youth, but she still has the capacity to walk.

I commented to her, very carefully and gently, that her problem was not an inability to walk. It seemed to me she was making her life miserable because she couldn't let go of wishing she could walk as easily as before.

As soon as Florence's mind had begun relating to her intense desire for things to be different, life for her had become miserable. She had felt overwhelmed by self-pity, anger, and fear. Florence and I tried to identify what she might be able to do to break out of that thinking pattern and learn to live with her impaired ability to walk. Florence was guardedly receptive.

Florence had trapped herself in self-made prison— always wishing for things to be different. It's a jail of the highest and most effective order and is a sure formula for intense suffering. In fact, a constant longing for life to be different is an excellent definition of suffering. We undermine our life process in this constant longing for things to be different. Desiring things we don't have, or endlessly worrying about the things we do have, absolutely contaminates all the good with which we are blessed.

This unsatisfiable wish for things to be different is at the very heart of mind*less*ness. Its opposite is embodied in the Law of Mindfulness.

ONE OF MY FAVORITE ACTIVITIES is listening to music. I love to hook up the headphones, put on a great piece of music, and turn up the volume. I become lost in the experience.

My attention is fully with the orchestra or vocalist. I feel exuberant. Other thoughts fade away. I'm living in the moment. My mind is happy and at peace.

This seems to last a maximum of about fifteen or twenty minutes. Then my mind kicks in: "You've got work to do. You've been promising to fix the garage door for two months. And you need to prepare for the presentation next week in Houston. What about your commitment to spend more time with the family?

"And how are you doing on funding Erica's college education? Hey, fella. How can you sit here wasting your time and your life listening to music? Get busy!"

What happened? Mindlessness. No longer in the moment, my mind is off and running. Does this ever happen to you? Of course it does, daily.

Mindfulness means being truly present with life and allowing it to unfold without judging it. This does not mean one does not set, move toward, and achieve goals. But it means that the actual achievement is secondary to the moment-to-moment experience of pursuing the goals. That requires a massive change in attitude.

A true story. My father-in-law visits. He notices the furnace isn't kicking out air like it should and suggests we have a look at the blower.

There are few things I dislike more in life than chores around the home. Yard work? Forget it. Painting? Not me. Furnace maintenance? No way. But here I am, prone on the basement floor, receiving instructions from my father-in-law on how to disconnect the blower belt.

All the time the thoughts are racing through my mind. "Why am I doing this? Greg, you promised yourself you wouldn't do this sort of thing. Hell, it was Dad's idea. Why doesn't he do it?"

My anger builds with every turn of the wrench. "How did I let myself get hooked into this?" Finally, the belt comes off. As I pull out, a belch emits from the air duct. Black soot is everywhere. I cough. I spit. I'm covered. I'm furious.

At this point, there are several choices. But my rage blinds me. I hear myself yelling, "Look at this mess you got me in." The only thing I could see was disaster.

The Law of Mindfulness reminds us to focus on the journey, not the destination. Joy is found not in finishing an activity but in *doing* it. Become aware of all that is here now, and enjoy it. While this guideline may pose a real challenge to many type-A personalities, it's the essence and power of the Law of Mindfulness.

Mindfulness means finding the incredible in the commonplace. Being fully present with our food as we eat—really savoring it, really tasting the fresh basil over the pasta rather than thinking about other things—is an example of mindfulness.

The Law of Mindfulness asks us to discipline and train our minds to let go of worries and desires, returning to these concerns when the actual moment has come to do something about them. In this way we can know happiness.

My wife saved the day in my furnace-fixing adventure. She heard the ruckus, came downstairs, and burst into laughter. In less than a minute, she had everyone

laughing at the absurd scene. She helped me realize
I had many choices. My response did not have to be
dictated by some mindless rage.

The Law of Mindfulness draws our consciousness
to a central choice: we have the power to determine
what we focus our attention on. Will it be the half of
the glass that is empty or the half of the glass that is full?
In that choice lies either suffering or contentment.

The Law of Mindfulness would have us understand
the difference between reasons and results. When we
don't have what we truly want in life — that is, the results — we usually have a long list of perfectly understandable reasons *why*. The mindless approach here is
to focus again and again on the "reasonable reasons"
that things aren't as we would choose.

The Law of Mindfulness suggests another approach.
Stop the mindless wishing that things would be different. Rather than wasting time and emotional and spiritual energy in explaining why we don't have what we
want, we can start to pursue other ways to get it.

Even our first baby steps in the right direction
are to be celebrated. Mindfulness says, "I will become
aware of my thoughts, I will exercise my power to
choose my thoughts, and I will choose thoughts that
bring happiness and contentment."

A friend of mine was in a tragic auto accident. She
was bringing a carload of kids back from a basketball

game when her car hit a patch of ice, went out of control, and slammed into a tree. Two of her daughter's classmates riding in the car were killed.

Understandably, Cindy went into a deep depression. As she lay in the hospital, suffering from multiple fractures herself, the thought of suicide came to her mind again and again: "I couldn't live with myself. How can you exist when you realize you are responsible for taking the lives of two young children?"

The cycle of "I'm at fault—I'm no good—I don't deserve to live" intensified. Cindy could find no peace of mind. She was trapped.

Wisely, her doctor prescribed counseling. A psychiatrist agreed to work with Cindy on becoming mindful. "Just be" was the advice from her more-experienced guide. Together they worked on calming her mind by having her center on her breathing. Cindy would let out a sigh of release. Then she would focus her attention on her breathing. She would "just be" as she concentrated her thoughts on a breath in and a breath out.

As Cindy's mind wandered, she learned to simply observe and follow those thoughts. Her guide helped her distinguish between negative thoughts, neutral thoughts, and nurturing thoughts.

Cindy's negative thoughts were typically regrets like "Why didn't I go slower that night?" and "Why couldn't I have died instead of the kids?" They got a rise out of Cindy every time, producing thoughts of guilt and shame. Most of these thoughts came automatically. Much of her time was spent locked in this mindless and destructive trap.

Cindy also discovered she had another group of thoughts: "Should I try my physical therapy?"; "I wonder what's on television." These thoughts would come and go frequently and didn't seem to matter all that much. They were the neutral thoughts.

Then Cindy discovered a third type of thought, the nurturing kind. While these thoughts did not come automatically, they were very helpful. She learned she could choose those thoughts—actively seek out and find a mind-set that would support her greater well-being.

Her favorite nurturing thought was "The Lord is my shepherd." This reflected her early childhood religious training and was a source of great comfort to her. Cindy progressed and found she could "catch" her thoughts as they drifted toward the negative. Then she would substitute a thought that would nourish. And she would visualize in her mind's eye being protected by a shepherd.

As Cindy became more skilled at this, she was amazed to discover that her depression and suicidal thoughts did not spring full-blown from nowhere. There were certain patterns she fell into that kept her thoughts of suicide going. When she learned to control her thoughts, her chronic depression disappeared.

This is a perfect demonstration of the Law of Mind-fulness. It is possible to break the automatic cycle. And when we do, we know wellness on a higher level.

Mindfulness means being really present with a hundred simple daily activities. It's an openness to the experience of taking a walk, really listening to the birds, feeling the gravel underfoot, hearing the wind through the pines.

When I am home, my daily walk takes me by a day-care center. Parents bring their kids early, and many youngsters head right for the huge sandbox. It's a joy to spend a moment watching them. The experience of the sand and the shovels and the pails is all fresh and new to the children, every day. Mindfulness would have us see that freshness and newness in our own daily life experiences.

Ultimately, we want the mind to become our servant rather than our master. It can become just that as we become aware of our thoughts in the present moment and make simple efforts to choose them.

Choose where you focus, and focus on thoughts that nurture. Concentrate on what you have, not what you've lost. You'll see the results in your health and your life.

It's all part of the non-negotiable Law of Mindfulness.

14

The Law of
Creativity

Imagination is the eye of the soul.

—*Joseph Joubert*

Everything is created twice—first mentally, then physically.

A blueprint precedes construction. A business plan comes before business success. Character development prefaces responsible and self-disciplined children. The first creation is on the mental plane; the physical result follows.

It's the non-negotiable Law of Creativity.

We use the law all the time, but seldom do we use it consciously. It's a principle that applies everywhere.

My wife is an amateur seamstress. As I write this, she is working on a new outfit for our daughter. In the creative process, she first has an idea for a colorful jumper. She and my daughter talk about colors. Then they select a pattern. Next it's time for material. Now the buttons. Every step is preceded by its mental equivalent. The physical follows the mental.

This is the Law of Creativity. Everything is created twice.

This simple and powerful principle applies to every area of life. Our parents come to visit and want to select a different, more scenic route home, something that will keep them away from the big cities. We get out the map; locate the starting point, their destination, a stop-over for the evening; and plan the entire route—all mental activity to this point. Then the day arrives for them to actually begin travel and the mental work is transformed into a physical reality. The thought precedes the deed.

The law is omnipresent. We recently did some landscaping; first we drew a plan. Our neighbors plant a large vegetable garden each year; Bob lays it out on paper first. Mental work. I create a speech first mentally, with the "take-away" message clearly in mind. The principle of two creations is constantly at work.

The Law of Creativity may seem so self-evident as to be unimportant. Beware. Do not be lulled into complacency or dismiss the power of this law. The potential for massive transformation resides here. For while it is true that all things are created twice, not all creations are conscious. And this is where our complacency can get us into deep trouble.

The Law of Creativity comes into play either by default or by design—by accident or on purpose. The trouble is, most often we simply react; we are passive. We accept what is without a single thought of what might be. We allow others to press our creative buttons.

Think back and connect with the Law of Personal Accountability. We each have an ability to respond, a power to create. This is not reaction. It is proaction, an idea that is intimately tied to the Law of Creativity.

Look at our personal lives. When we do not accept personal responsibility and do not develop awareness of the tremendously powerful Law of Creativity, we empower other people to set the agendas of our lives. Circumstances tend to shape our lives by default, not by choice.

Design or default—a key criterion for understanding the Law of Creativity. For instance, a life script may have been handed to us by our parents. We respond out of habit, obligation, or even coercion. By default, without conscious thought, we find ourselves in a life of someone else's choosing.

William Taylor found himself in a preparatory school and then in an Ivy League college, headed for Harvard Law. "My father was an attorney, a partner in a large Wall Street firm, and very successful by his standards. But that was the last thing I wanted to do. Three days before I was to matriculate at Harvard, I told my dad I wasn't going. He came unglued. But I stuck to my dream. Today we have a great life in the north country of Idaho."

Think about first creations: a father creating a life for a son; a son rejecting the father's dream and following his own. In both cases, the idea—the first creation—precedes the reality. Take charge of our own agendas and we creatively shape our own lives.

William risked big-time. He knew there would be resistance from his parents, maybe even total rejection and no inheritance. But he was willing to challenge the script that was being handed him by his family. William felt he had to shape his life by his own design. Default would never have been acceptable.

The Law of Creativity would have us challenge the scripts that are everywhere in our lives. Whether we see it or not, there is a first creation at work all the time. Who we are and what circumstances we experience are second creations. Those second creations either are a product of our own design or come from other people's agendas, from unchallenged circumstances, or from our own unexamined personal habits.

The good news is that the Law of Creativity shows us an incredibly powerful way to shape our experience of life. Through our unique human capacities of self-awareness and imagination, we can take charge and learn to fashion our own first creations.

I have had the good fortune of knowing and working with Robert Schuller, the founder of the Crystal Cathedral Ministries. His concept of "possibility thinking" has yielded positive changes in countless lives throughout the world. The very word *possibility* releases a mental climate conducive to creativity. I have seen the simple suggestion that something is possible release creative thinking and break the invisible and limiting prisons of difficult circumstance and deep despair.

Wilbert was in a severe work accident. A tree fell on him and broke his back. He was paralyzed from the waist down. The doctors told him he'd never walk again. But Wil felt it was possible to strive for recovery. "In my mind," he said, "I saw myself walking again. In my mind, I saw myself exercising every day. In my mind, I saw myself happy, making a contribution to family and society."

Wil's first team of doctors told him he would be living his life confined to a wheelchair. But they did not understand who Wil was or what motivated him. They did not recognize that Wil could use the Law of Creativity to help himself, that he was filled with possibilities.

Wil envisioned working his legs, moving them in rhythmic motions so the muscles would not forget their movement. With the help of a creative physical therapist, Wil fashioned a unique bicycle he could strap to his legs and pedal while lying on his back. Wil used his arms to keep the legs moving, pushing and pulling his knees, all the time envisioning himself walking.

Soon he was able to sit erect. Then he wanted to mount a stationary bicycle. With some creative thought, Wil sketched a handrail that would keep him stable while on the bicycle. He strapped his feet to the pedals and away he pedaled. Wil added time at the whirlpool bath, worked with leg weights, and did upper-body exercises.

Today, he's walking with the help of a walker. What's next? "I'm going to get to a cane by the first of the year."

Many principles are at work in Wil's journey toward wellness. But the Law of Creativity governs them all. The first creation, thought, precedes the second creation, physical reality. Possibilities abound when the mind is set free to create.

To understand the link between creativity and possibilities, consider their antonym, that nasty ten-letter word *impossible*. Utter this word and the effect is devastating. Thinking stops. Progress is halted. Doors slam shut.

Think "impossible" and dreams get discarded, projects get abandoned, and hope for wellness is torpedoed. But let someone yell the words "It's possible," and resources we hadn't been aware of come rushing in to assist us in our quest. I believe we are all potentially brilliant and creative — but only if we believe it, only if we have an attitude of positive expectancy toward our ideas, and only if we act on them.

The fact is, we can rescript our lives. We can engage the Law of Creativity and become our own first creator.

Pete wanted to lose weight, lots of it: 150 pounds. First, Pete became self-aware. This meant recognizing his problem and affirming a deeply held conviction that high-quality life was a gift he wanted to enjoy as long as possible.

Pete also became aware that his eating was a way of handling unfulfilled emotional needs. When he overate, he was living out a script that was not in harmony with the values he believed in. The way Pete was living his life was not the product of his own proactive design, but the result of a first-creation habit learned from his mother, who constantly met her emotional needs through food.

"I realized I could change," said Pete. "I determined to live out of my own life rather than out of the memory of how my mother coped."

Change Pete did! Over a period of seven months, Pete lost over ninety pounds. He is still on his program of a vegetarian diet coupled with exercise. Pete is scripting himself around his limitless potential instead of his limiting past. He has become his own first creator.

That's the Law of Creativity. The vision precedes the reality.

What this law says is that the imagining facility is the creative facility. It is necessary for us to see an idea in our mind's eye before it can become reality. The right brain, the creative and limitless side of the mind, is engaged. The left brain, the cognitive and linear side, takes second chair.

The Law of Creativity asks us not to mandate our future. Instead, the law asks us to seek the divine design in our lives. As we'll learn in discussing the Law of Life Mission, few people have the faintest idea of what their divine and most creative design is.

I believe one should not visualize or force a mental picture. Thousands of people have been disappointed by doing so and, as a result, have come to mistrust the

Law of Creativity. Instead, let the divine design come naturally and intuitively. It's there if we'll listen.

Mozart and Beethoven both said they heard symphonies in their heads, and had only to write them down. The Law of Creativity.

Begin to see yourself making great progress. But don't press or drive the creative force. You and I need to be the ones to conform to the Law of Creativity rather than expecting the law to conform to our contrived needs.

The divine plan found through the Law of Creativity does, I believe, include things like health, ample supply, love, and perfect self-expression. The law brings happiness, albeit a happiness we may not have consciously chosen. In fact, the Law of Creativity may bring great changes to life, for nearly everyone has wandered far from the divine design.

As an eleven-year-old boy, the pioneering aeronautical engineer Igor Sikorsky recorded a dream he had in which he was inside a big flying ship, one that he built himself. About thirty years later, Sikorsky lived that dream as Charles Lindbergh piloted one of his "flying boats." In his mid-fifties, Sikorsky developed the helicopter. In both dramatic cases, the mental creation precedes the reality.

The Law of Creativity calls not for my way or your way, but for the best way. This is the picture, the idea we must find and hold on to without wavering. Then we create wellness in body, mind, and spirit, wellness of the highest level.

Following my experience with cancer, I let go of my willful ways and was able to surrender, with sincerity, to God's way. Out of that surrender came a vision of service to others, something that was never in my life formula before. I've held on to that picture. As a result, my life has been used in ways I'd never have dreamed possible. The vision leads the fact. The Law of Creativity is at work.

All things are created twice. First the mental creation, and then the physical counterpart. What are you holding in your mind? Ask for the divine design, and hold fast to that vision.

You'll be experiencing the power of the non-negotiable Law of Creativity.

15

The Law of
Lifetime Growth

We must always change, renew, rejuvenate
ourselves; otherwise we harden.

—*Goethe*

The most up-to-date research in gerontology has uncovered a shocking conclusion: as much as 80 percent of what we now call "old age" is not related to biology. Instead, it has its roots in expectations and attitudes. True, the 20 percent that is a product of biology may incapacitate us and even result in our death. But the good news is this: if we concentrate on improving and changing the unnecessary 80 percent, we stand to profit beyond our most optimistic expectations.

The Law of Lifetime Growth is at the heart of this approach.

Everyone—young, old, rich, poor, healthy, diseased—absolutely everyone has the capacity to change, to learn, to evolve, and to grow.

Yet we succumb to a set of cultural beliefs that classify and restrict people to roles that create anything but total wellness. It's high time to take seriously the Law of Lifetime Growth.

I was fortunate to be raised in a household that treasured lifetime growth. It was important in our home that we all had an understanding of world news—not just the story, but the history and the people behind the stories. My mother and father made us think. What were the alternatives to a border fight in Pakistan? How could inflation be kept in check? What about civil rights in our own state?

We were encouraged to read, to study, to think for ourselves. In both high school and college I was active in speaking and debate. My parents encouraged me to choose topics that stretched the mind and challenged the thinking and then to reduce those subjects to clearly understandable terms that anyone could grasp. Since the earliest days, I was primed for lifetime growth. Today, I have an insatiable curiosity.

The Law of Lifetime Growth is inextricably inter-twined with the idea of vital curiosity. It works for children, young adults, career trackers, and seniors. The idea is to constantly explore, to seek, to have an attitude and bearing that says, "I'm interested in finding out what life holds."

Lifetime growth is much more than a classroom issue. Its boundaries spread far beyond academe. Lifetime growth is the cornerstone of successful parenting, of career satisfaction—of fulfillment in all of life.

Nowhere do I need the Law of Lifetime Growth more critically than in my work with senior citizens. In our programs at retirement communities, we view with a critical eye any activities that aim to pacify the residents. Such activities come out of a kind of baby-sitting model of elder care; they create dependency.

I bristled when one social director recently described her intent as "to keep the natives quiet."

Such attitudes stand as cultural roadblocks to lifetime growth. We limit and categorize people based on age and our own beliefs about aging. Our words betray a deep cynicism regarding older people: "Old means no longer productive"; "A senior citizen should just enjoy the golden years"; "He has earned a rest."

No more! The Law of Lifetime Growth must come to the forefront. This law is a far-reaching idea, one that shakes the very foundations of modern society. And it is filled with promise.

Governments and citizens must commit to the concept of lifetime growth. We must recognize that growth is *always* possible, no matter what our age or ability. Are disabilities limiting? Sometimes. Is growth still possible? Of course. We must redouble our efforts to honor the potential of each life throughout its span.

This law is violated constantly at every level of society. To put an end to this, we must shift the beliefs of massive numbers of people in all cultures. We must strike the category of age off documents except for statistical and record-keeping purposes, in the same manner that the Constitution prohibits us from discriminating on the basis of race or religion. No person should ever again be forced to retire simply because of age.

A commitment to lifetime growth is the key.

Attitude-altering attempts are not the exclusive domain of government. Ultimately, we are each responsible for creating and satisfying our curiosity about life. Our efforts make all the difference! The list of great men and women who have committed themselves to this law is long and inspiring.

Thomas Alva Edison, who attended school for only three months and was deemed mentally slow by his teachers, patented a total of 1,033 inventions! His work spanned a lifetime, with his first patent issued at age twenty-one, his last at age eighty-one. Much of the technology of the twentieth century derives from his achievements, of which the electric light bulb and the generation of electricity are but two.

The lessons: genius does not depend on advanced degrees or the approval of others; pursue your God-given talents throughout your life. That's the Law of Lifetime Growth.

The comedian George Burns, born on New York's Lower East Side, after the death in 1964 of his beloved wife, Gracie Allen, was expected to retire. Instead, he became even more involved in his work and in life. At the age of eighty he won an Oscar for his role in *The Sunshine Boys*. He's booked to play Las Vegas on his hundredth birthday. That's lifetime growth.

The lessons: overcome loss; rise to new and greater possibilities; never let age be an excuse. That's the Law of Lifetime Growth.

Anna Mary Moses, better known as Grandma Moses, the much-loved painter, farmed until her late seventies. For many of her years she also embroidered, but when she turned seventy-eight her fingers had become too stiff to handle a needle; she began to paint in oils instead. Her pictures of rural America were soon on exhibit internationally. In the hundredth year of her life, she illustrated an edition of *A Visit from St. Nicholas* (" 'Twas the night before Christmas . . ."); it was published in 1962, one year after her death.

The lesson: keep seeking even after defeat. Your greatest work may yet lie ahead. That's the Law of Lifetime Growth.

George Bernard Shaw, the British playwright, remained active and immensely productive until his death at ninety-four. A seminal thinker who sparked thoughtful debate, Shaw wrote about the arts and politics, penning his last play when he was in his late eighties. His work has stood the test of time.

The lesson: cultivate ideas. Respond to issues that intrigue and motivate. Pursue these interests daily. That's the Law of Lifetime Growth.

The social anthropologist Margaret Mead, at age seventy-two, made a trip to study the Arapesh people of New Guinea. In 1975, a television documentary traced a typical week in her life. She was constantly busy — contributing and exploring. Her week was so packed with work that it exhausted the television crew, most of whom were less than half her age.

The lesson: find your passion and pursue it. That's the Law of Lifetime Growth.

Benjamin Franklin, writer, scientist, inventor, and one of the greatest statesmen of the Revolutionary era, achieved his most notable victories in later life. At seventy, he was a member of the committee that drafted the Declaration of Independence, as well as one of its signers. He was seventy-five when he negotiated the end to the War of Independence. Called the wisest American, Franklin was eighty-one when he effected the compromise that brought the Constitution of the United States into being.

The lessons: work, contribute, find a higher cause, give of self, and devote your life to the well-being of others. The qualities that drove such activities did not disappear when Franklin died. Perhaps they are out of style. But the great life can be ours by pursuing those ideals. That's the Law of Lifetime Growth.

Edward "Duke" Ellington never retired—although he "retired from booze" when he was in his mid-forties. For nearly fifty years he had a band, always performing, circling the globe. He made his first recording in 1924 and his last in 1974, not many weeks before his death. He left a great legacy—the most distinctive single body of composition in the history of jazz.

The lessons: never retire—except to put personal excesses to rest. Always aspire—for the greater goal. That's the Law of Lifetime Growth.

The Law of Lifetime Growth demands both a cultural change and a megashift in our own thinking about all life can be.

This law of wellness represents a great hope for people of all ages, all states of wellness, all cultures.

Grow. Learn. Pursue. Contribute. Enjoy. Make the commitment. You'll know fulfillment as never before. It's the non-negotiable Law of Lifetime Growth.

Part Six

The Vocational Laws

16

The Law of
Life Mission

He dies every day who lives a lingering life.

—Pierrard Poullet

Conventional wisdom says, "If you have your health, you have everything." Don't believe it. It's not so much that this old adage is wrong as that there is a higher truth.

The Law of Life Mission holds, "If you have a purpose, you have everything."

Purpose. Your life's mission. Your reason for existing. This law asks us to consider our great aim—the work we have been brought on this earth to do.

Everyone has a unique life mission. There is for each and every person a perfect self-expression. This consists of the role he or she is to fill. Finding this self-expression is a task no one else can accomplish; it is something special to you and to me. This is personal destiny!

If we intend to experience total wellness, discovering and following our unique purpose is mandatory.

The problem: most people haven't the faintest notion of what their life mission is. The typical person, busy living what looks like a productive life, may be as far away from her or his true life mission as north is from south. Yet all the time a marvelous plan lies hidden deep within.

Millions upon millions of people have paid a high price for violating this law—always wondering, never fulfilled. Life satisfaction eludes them.

The Law of Life Mission demands that the genius within each of us be released. The perfect plan does exist. We must search diligently and continuously until that plan is clear. Settle for anything less and we will be disappointed.

Roger Burtonelli's dramatic transformation came when he discovered his mission. Diagnosed with metastatic lymphoma, he was confined to his room, receiving morphine intravenously in order to manage his pain. I visited Roger and in the middle of our conversation felt led to ask, "What's your mission?"

He was puzzled. "Well," I continued, "You're a man of great wisdom. Do you think you need to share that with others?"

Roger was silent. "What do you have in mind?" he finally asked, slowly and deliberately.

"I can't be sure," I replied. "But let me ask, have you shared the lessons you've learned in your rich and full life with your grandchildren?"

What happened next is something I have seen repeatedly in people who catch a vision of their mission. Roger's face visibly brightened. His skin color went from ashen gray to vibrant pink. His whole demeanor began to make a shift. His posture changed: he'd been slumping over, and now he was sitting nearly erect in his chair. A smile came to his lips. He held his head high. He raised an arm as he spoke.

"I could write them letters," he smiled. "That's something I'm able to do."

Roger started his writing mission. Each letter addressed one subject. The first was on persistence. The next, on the value of reading. Another, on how to handle failure.

Roger began to feel better.

Other letters followed—on true success, personal efficiency, happiness, and friendship.

Roger needed less morphine.

I phoned. "I think God has a plan for me right here in these letters," said Roger. "This is not labor, it's play."

One of the certain signs we're living life "on purpose" is that our labors are of such absorbing interest that they seem almost like play. When we find time passing unusually quickly, we can be sure the activity in which we're engrossed is related in some way to our purpose.

Roger called about six months later. "I have twenty-three letters, each on a different subject. And I feel like my health is the best it's been in over two years."

Roger continues to write to this day. He asked me to help him contact a publisher because he believes he has a book in the making. I agree.

PURPOSE! Mission!

The Law of Life Mission has power we don't understand.

Despite the evidence of its power, most people continue to violate this law. We are influenced by our parents in our career choices. We look to counselors to give direction to our lives. Peer pressure and economic concerns determine our futures. Yet none of this may have anything to do with our life mission.

It's difficult to change a person's life path once its direction is established. But implicit in the Law of Life Mission is an eternal compass that is always calling us in the right direction, leading us to higher ground.

The Law of Life Mission encompasses health, wealth, love, and a perfect expression of personal potential. Its achievement brings happiness. Big promises all, but not impossible.

Many people believe that adversity, including life-threatening illness, has a message in it—a call to get their life back "on purpose," closer to their life mission.

In hindsight, I believe this was true in my experience of cancer. I learned the lesson firsthand from Mimi. Mimi's illness—a form of lupus, the degenerative auto-immune disease that brings with it fever, skin lesions, and arthritic changes—brought her face-to-face with the fact that she always put herself and her needs second. Everyone else—including her husband, her two sons, and her co-workers—came first.

She had given up her dream of living in Maine because her husband worked in the aerospace industry and the only opportunities were in Southern California. Her sons wanted to play sports, something Mimi had little interest in, yet she was expected to chauffeur them to all their sporting activities. She wanted to return to work in some church-related way. But she had accepted a part-time job in a mission for the homeless because the commute to a full-time job would have been too great.

It all added up to Mimi putting her life on hold for the benefit of others. Then lupus . . . at age forty-one.

Mimi was not doing well until she read about how illness can be a message to change, to get our lives back "on purpose." She began to respond to her life mission and today is a writer for a religious television show.

The message of illness: get our lives on purpose, back to fulfilling our mission.

Shelly was a highly successful writer. Her income topped a quarter of a million dollars a year for five years. But she despised the work. In Shelly's heart she knew this wasn't her mission. Her response? She went back to school and earned a master's degree in education. She was meant to be the best elementary school teacher she could be.

And that is precisely what she is doing today.

But listen carefully: a mission is not synonymous with a goal. A mission cannot be checked off and reached. A mission is fulfilled, continuously, in every moment. Goals that can be defined and obtained are only way stations along the road that is life's mission.

The Law of Life Mission calls us to invest our lives in unique ways. This raises the all-important question, How do I discover my life mission?

The most effective way I know to understand and clarify life purpose is to develop a personal mission statement. This is really a personal philosophy or creed, a statement unique to you that describes what you believe God wants you to do with your life.

In his book 7 *Habits of Highly Effective People*, Stephen Covey encourages us to consider our mission in three distinct areas. First, focus on what we want to be: our character. Next, consider what we want to do: our contributions and achievements. Finally, consider the values and principles upon which our character and contributions are based: our life "center."

The Law of Life Mission calls us to get in touch with this center. Each of us has a center, although we usually don't recognize it as such. It's the lens through which we filter all our life experiences, the north star by which we navigate.

People build their lives around all manner of centers. There are career centers, family centers, hobby centers, and goal centers. There are health centers, money centers, power centers, recognition centers, possession centers, friend centers, enemy centers, church centers, and, of course, self-centers.

What stands at your center? Sometimes it isn't that easy to see. If career is at the center, you'll be driven to produce at the sacrifice of health, relationships, and other important areas of life. I know a woman who is enemy centered, her life consumed by the perceived injustices of her ex-husband. At one time I was church centered, so caught up in the projects and programs of the organization that I became blind to my own needs. It's one of the reasons I nearly died from lung cancer.

Recognize that you do have a center. Perhaps it's leisure—a quest responsible for many premature deaths. Maybe it's fun—a path filled with deep holes. Detach, and view your life for a moment to discover your center. What drives you? What is of prime importance?

Answering these questions with sincerity is the core work of wellness. The Law of Life Mission demands this work of us. And from this effort flow the character and contributions of our lives.

What distinctive attributes, ethical traits, and personal reputation will you shape for yourself? Living a life of integrity is one of the greatest missions we can undertake. What contributions will you make? Maybe you'll bring up a child in an atmosphere of love. Perhaps you'll serve others through your talents in music. Maybe your mission is to correct an oppressive social condition.

For most of us, no dramatic shift is required; we'll probably find all the mission opportunities we need within a ten-minute drive of our front door. You probably won't have to move or change jobs. Bloom where you are planted! What is required is a vision of a great calling, a sense that we are becoming all we were meant to be. That comes from within.

Our lives can be powerfully shaped by what we long to become. I believe the dream of what might be is more important than the record of what has been. We must, however, be serious about that vision.

For me to feel the deep personal satisfaction of living life on purpose, I needed a sense that my unique life mission was inspired by God. Once I found that sense, I became seriously determined about pursuing the dream. And through that pursuit, I have found more fulfillment than I ever imagined.

It's the Law of Life Mission.

What is comes from what may be as well as what has been. Seek mission.

The truth is that our highest and greatest well-being is dependent on giving and sharing. Mission is not about what comes back; it is about what goes out.

Become keenly aware of what's going out. It's the key to successfully applying the non-negotiable Law of Life Mission.

17

The Law of
Purpose Through Service

Try not to become a man of success,
but rather try to become a man of value.

—Albert Einstein

The first cousin of the Law of Life Mission is the Law of Purpose Through Service.

Mission comes alive only through service—the idea of caring for others. There's magic in this law. When we serve with depth and sincerity, we get a glimpse of the essential quality of who we really can become.

We may be sitting alone, lost in self-doubt or mired in self-pity, our troubles seeming to overwhelm us. The phone rings. It's a friend who's really in need. Without conscious thought, we break out of our self-imposed shell of isolation.

We listen. We give words of assurance. We serve. When we put the phone down, who feels better? The friend does, we hope. But we do, too! And when we reflect on what took place, we understand more clearly who we really are and what we have to offer others. We know a new level of wellness.

What's at work here is the Law of Purpose Through Service.

The best way we can fulfill—in fact, the only way of fulfilling—our highest wellness potential is through service to others. Success in life is measured not by longevity or wealth or honors or power. Those people on the wellness journey measure success by service, by the degree to which we've helped others. Benjamin Franklin, America's Renaissance man, lived and breathed the Law of Purpose Through Service. He once said he owed his happiness to the philosophy he had formulated half a century earlier, which he summarized: "The most acceptable service to God is doing good to man." History is filled with examples of people, even heads of state, who counted themselves failures although they had shown great skill at accumulating riches and power.

No matter what our vocation, whether we are the president of the United States or a mucker of horse stalls, unless we can approach our duty with a deep sense of purpose, we will never find satisfaction. Fulfillment will forever elude us. Even when we are cleaning a horse stall, the attitude of serving others, of caring for God's creation, can shine through. Then we know contentment.

How can I serve? is a profound question in everyone's wellness equation. The assumptions behind it are critically important for the serious wellness student. We must think through, personalize, and understand both intellectually and emotionally this idea of finding purpose through helping others.

The truth is, we are here to serve. Marianne Williamson, in her book *A Return to Love*, wrote about her search through many spiritual and philosophical writings: "It felt as though they led me up a huge flight of stairs to a giant cathedral inside my mind. But once I reached the top of the stairs, the door to the church was locked." Then she found the key that opened the door. "The key, very simply, is other people."

That's it! It's the Law of Purpose Through Service. We find our purpose with others.

How can I serve? What can I contribute? Where can I give? How can I demonstrate I care? Who needs my love? What life journeys have I successfully navigated, and how can I share my experience and insights with others? In the answers to these questions lies purpose that is directly tied to serving others.

This law asks that we examine our motivation for service. It does not demand that we serve. There can be little esprit, the all-important first law of wellness, when we are mandated to action. Instead, we become sincerely motivated to action.

The Law of Purpose Through Service asks that we make a habit of helping others, so that helping becomes for us a natural way of expressing compassion. The law challenges us to live out life's greatest equation: in Emerson's words, "You cannot sincerely help another without helping yourself."

Understand that the Law of Purpose Through Service is a two-way street. We fulfill our purpose through serving the next person. The reward? We enhance and enrich our own life through that service. Note the order: first we serve; then we are enriched. It's a wonderful covenant.

The law's promise compels us to choose to let our compassion for others come forth in a spontaneous manner because it is our deepest and best nature to do so. Able to serve and help in ways we never before imagined, we discover an inner joy and contentment in everything we do.

OUR FAMILY had friends who were living very near the epicenter of California's 1994 Northridge earthquake. Their beautiful home collapsed. The great wood beams that once supported the cathedral ceiling of the warm and inviting living room now lay smashed in front of the fireplace. The home's foundation revealed cracks large enough to stick your fist through. The bedroom wing of the house was starting to inch its way downhill.

Our friends were terrified. The realization that they had lost most of their material possessions left them devastated. Tears flowed. They could focus only on their loss.

They were unable to work that first week following the quake. They would get up early, leave their hotel room, and sort through the pile of rubble that was once their home. Neighbors would come, some to help, some to share their misery. My friend, an attorney, found himself counseling them and giving guidance, an activity that gave him great satisfaction. "Where do I file a claim?" "How do I get a disaster-relief loan?" "What can I do about my insurance company?" Working at a card table set up on his street, he started to help others.

"I have never felt more satisfaction in my entire life," he told me recently. "I want to do more of this, to help where I'm needed. We're probably not going to rebuild the big home. It took too much of our time to maintain, time better used in service to those who can really use a hand."

WHEN WE SERVE, our idea of the nature of helping expands. We grow, and are of even greater service as a result. And we know inner peace and joy.

This is the real benefit and reward of consciously practicing the Law of Purpose Through Service: an opportunity to help relieve suffering in another while growing in character ourselves.

But there are clearly many ways in which we hesitate to serve. Or we get confused when we try. I used to serve in the middle of downtown Los Angeles. Every day a different stranger would ask, "Can you spare a quarter?" And every day I would witness certain biases surfacing within me. I would hesitate. I would think of reasons not to help.

I first held back because I felt the works of compassion had become somewhat formalized. I put money in the collection plate. I gave at the office. Those funds had been, or should have been, put to use for this person already. If not, I would rationalize, they're waiting for him, in one form or another, at the local rescue mission. And that day no quarter would make its way from my pocket to meet his need.

I'd get angry at God. Looking at the squalor these people lived in, I'd cry out, "God, can't you see? Don't you care? Won't you do something about it?" Then the answer came. "Yes, I do see. Yes, I do care. And yes, I am doing something about it because I have just brought their problem to your attention."

One time, it seemed certain that the fellow asking for money was an alcoholic. "If you give him money, you're crazy," my friends would say. "You're only feeding his habit, digging his grave deeper, adding to the woes he already has."

One day I brought two sandwiches from home, beautifully prepared: tuna salad and lettuce on whole-wheat bread. I thought I'd give them to the fellow instead of money. He looked at the bag of sandwiches, gave them to the man standing next to him, and shouted to the next person coming down the sidewalk, "Hey, buddy, can you spare a quarter?"

My instinctive reaction was to feel that I had been treated unfairly. "Hey, where's your gratitude?" I wanted to shout. But as a friend later reminded me, purpose is found through service, and service must be offered totally, without conditions of acceptance.

An important lesson. No conditions. The Law of Purpose Through Service has its simple side and its complex side. The laws of wellness are not always easy.

The choice of *how* to serve forced me to examine my motives and consider my own needs. I had expected appreciation, some sort of positive reinforcement. When I uncovered the hidden conditions that I had attached to helping another person, I was truly surprised. I had been operating out of pride, out of a need for recognition; my ego needed strokes. I grew through that experience.

The Law of Purpose Through Service makes us face the essential question of personal motives. With a minimal amount of introspection and a reasonable amount of perspective, we can come to see many of our ego-driven motives as signals calling for our own personal growth. Once I was able to reduce my ego's influence, I was free to serve without regard to undue praise. My reward was in the act of serving itself, not in the psychological payback.

There are thousands of ways to serve. Visit a friend who's sick. Give someone a bouquet of flowers. Volunteer at your local Red Cross, Salvation Army, or Habitat for Humanity.

Telephone someone and give that person a lift. Send a card with a note of encouragement. Fix a snack and take it to a senior center. Paint a picture and give it away. Help at your church or synagogue. Invite friends over for a meal. Speak up at your local city council when you see an injustice. Volunteer at a hospital.

Write a personal history and make copies for all your family members. Plan a trip for your club to tour your state capitol building. Plant a tree or a rosebush. Help clean up an elderly neighbor's yard. Volunteer at a soup kitchen or homeless shelter. Be a secret pal to a friend for a week and drop off goodies or send a card and then identify yourself at the end of the week.

I smile when I consider all the possibilities.

The Law of Purpose Through Service. It's a wonderful and powerful law. We help another. We help ourselves. We find meaning. Our satisfaction soars. To top it off, we can even have a good time while we're doing it.

When we think of living the truly fulfilling life, let's think often of the non-negotiable Law of Purpose Through Service.

18

The Law of
Stewardship

If you want happiness for a lifetime—
help the next generation.

—*Chinese proverb*

The quest for personal wellness is an illusion without a commitment to the wellness of all and the entire universe. We do not stand alone. The people of this planet are interdependent in all things.

It's the Law of Stewardship, and it has us realize the interdependence of all things. Everything we do has an effect, either for good or for ill, on the wellness of ourselves and ultimately on the wellness of the Earth. Its mandate is revolutionary: we are called to live our lives with appropriate regard for others.

The implications of this law are massive, its application both simple and complex. For the Law of Stewardship calls for us to do nothing less than examine and awaken our conscience to see the connectedness of all of life.

We don't "own" anything. Not really. We may use something for a while. But we don't own it. We pass it along or discard it.

Not one thing is ours in terms of absolute ownership.

But you say, "Wait, here's the title to my car. I own it." According to the legal system, yes. But we are actually users of that asset for a period of time. Then we pass it on.

"But, my house. It's mine free and clear. Look at the deed." Same concept. We may use it, even over our entire lifetime. It may stay in the family through several generations. But we don't own it in a real sense; we are users.

"I created this business from scratch, from nothing but an idea on a scrap of paper. You can't possibly tell me this isn't mine." Well, it isn't. Legally, you and the bank may be registered and responsible. But it's a myth that this asset is really yours, or even your heirs'. We may even assign a dollar value to the asset and sell it. But even those dollars aren't really ours.

The concept of ownership is dwarfed by this larger idea called stewardship. Here the emphasis is on the deep responsibility we each have to leave this world in a better condition than it was in when we arrived.

Nowhere is the need for the role of stewardship more evident than in our awakening ecological consciousness. Stewardship of the planet joins forces that are economic, social, vocational, legal, political, medical, aesthetic, and spiritual.

The Law of Stewardship requires us to pass the planet on to future generations in a better condition than we found it in. Historically, we have not done well in this area. The required restoration will touch every aspect of the way we live—from our purchases to the size of families we choose to our choices in leisure activities.

The old school said, "Eat, drink, and be merry." The new school says, "Eat, drink, and be merry, as long as lifestyle and consumption decisions demonstrate wise use of limited resources."

There's a group of people in northern California who desire to form a fifty-first state. Their goal is to divide California in half and create, in their half, a model economic and political system where stewardship would be the first concern.

However farfetched that may sound, the values this group espouses are based in stewardship. They seek to bring together the best of the high-technology culture while simultaneously renewing their commitment to providing a high quality of life and long-term vocational, recreational, and intellectual opportunities.

Listen to the pained and defensive cries of the politicians, particularly those from southern California. They recognize that this proposal is based on vastly more than a concern for the redwoods. The intent is to exponentially improve life quality, for this generation and the next and the next and the next. The awakened consciousness of stewardship is at the core.

But we don't have to be part of a movement to form a new state in order to know the power of the Law of Stewardship. In our own homes and at our daily places of business, the role of steward takes on immediacy. Are we teaching our children values based on appropriate consumption, conservation, permanency, recycling, quality, craftsmanship—all based on meeting authentic needs? Or are we still promoting mindless consumption, planned obsolescence, and the satisfaction of advertising's artificially created "needs"?

The Law of Stewardship asks for personal change.

At home, for instance, I am careful to use only the water I need to rinse my razor when I'm shaving. But one morning on a recent trip away from home, I let the water run as I shaved. It didn't take my daughter more than a minute to say, "Dad, you're wasting the planet's resources." At least some of our efforts to teach our daughter the concept of stewardship have worked.

Many people dismiss such small acts as irrelevant. Not so! When, not if, we couple the Law of Stewardship with the Law of Personal Accountability, all our small, practical everyday acts will create a synergy that will contribute to our own wellness and the earth's at the same time!

Opportunities for stewardship are everywhere. Maybe we'll make a commitment to plant a million new urban trees. With this simple act, which would be undertaken by hundreds of thousands of our neighbors as well, we would add to the aesthetic value of our urban environments, save billions of dollars in electricity, contribute to the refoliation of the earth, and boost the health and quality of life of millions of people, now and in the future. That's stewardship.

I LIVED in the Los Angeles area for over a decade. Shortly after moving there, I looked out one day to see my neighbor doing yard work with a surgical mask covering his mouth and nose. I thought he must be supersensitive or allergic to something like pollen or ragweed.

"No," he said, "I work for the South Coast Air Quality Management District. I know what's in this air. And I don't want any more of it in my lungs than is absolutely necessary."

I learned a great deal about the air-pollution problems of this region from my neighbor. Some of their causes are geographical, with mountains trapping the air, not allowing for any release. Other causes are industrial: for decades manufacturing, commercial, and industrial production facilities dumped toxic chemicals without regard for the future; others pumped solvents and ash into the air with impunity. For all the economic good industry contributed, it also contributed to some of the most unhealthy air of any major metropolitan area in the world.

Auto and truck traffic added to the problems. Southern California at one point actually made a decision to abandon mass transportation in favor of the now world-famous freeway system. For years the area "solved" its transportation problems by building more freeways. More freeways meant more cars meant housing developments in outlying communities meant longer commutes meant more hours in the car meant more pollution meant worse air meant more sickness meant. . . . It goes on and on. It's interdependent. Everything we do has an effect on all.

The Law of Stewardship asks us to think through these very decisions before we commit to their implementation. The Law of Stewardship demands that we undertake actions with proper and high regard for other people and the next generation.

A footnote on the Southern California air. My neighbor and his co-workers are making excellent progress. In the last ten years, first-stage smog alerts have plunged from over 100 per year to 23 per year. Less severe smog days have fallen from over 200 per year in 1980 to under 100 in 1994. The combination of a state auto emissions program, controls on refineries and factories, plus the introduction of new technologies including clean fuels, all played important roles in the turnaround. Stewardship does work.

The Law of Stewardship demands that we make shifts in our thinking and behavior. This is not a luxury; it's a necessity. When air becomes so toxic we must wear masks, when local water sources are so contaminated we must buy bottled water, when strip-mining devastates the beauty of a valley and the mining company accepts no responsibility for regenerating the landscape, when agricultural chemicals are traced to an incidence of lymphoma fourteen times the national rate, then it is time to seriously reevaluate our priorities.

The Law of Stewardship shows us that the planet on which we live has systems that regulate temperature, air flow, rainfall, and a whole host of other variables. The earth is much more than a chunk of rock with different species of plants and animals living on it. It is a highly complex system made up of many smaller systems, of which humankind is just one. Our place within these systems is as steward. Let's be certain we renew our renewable resources and conserve those not renewable. We are here to leave things better than when we found them.

The Law of Stewardship applies equally to the country's economic sphere. If we continue to operate under current beliefs and practices, we will saddle future generations with an overwhelming debt that will constrain life as we know it. Reducing the national debt, operating under a balanced budget, and ensuring economic growth are not partisan political agendas. They are economic imperatives of our time. We must leave our economy, just like the planet, better than we found it.

The Law of Stewardship also applies at work. We are under an obligation to contribute through our jobs to making life better for all. This closely parallels the

Law of Purpose Through Service. We must invest our work lives for the good of all.

Relationships? Of course the Law of Stewardship applies. We are each charged with building and encouraging one another.

The Law of Stewardship applies even on a spiritual level. Our life is not ours. Face it: life's a gift, given freely by the Ultimate Giver. As stewards, let's set out to make a return gift—the gift of our lives. It's all we can do in appreciation for all we have been given.

In the final analysis, the Law of Stewardship requires us to manage our lives in such a way that we hold in high regard the welfare of others and leave things better than when we found them. We are all stewards. Let's rise to meet our responsibilities.

Simple and profound. It's the non-negotiable Law of Stewardship.

Part Seven

The Spiritual Laws

19

The Law of
Forgiveness

Forgiveness restores our hearts to the
innocence that we knew—an innocence
that allowed us the freedom to love.

—*Robin Casarjian*
author of *Forgiveness: A Bold Choice*
for a Peaceful Heart

Forgiveness is one of the most beautiful words in the English language. Mark this as one of the great truths of the collective wisdom passed down through the centuries: life can be lived most abundantly as an adventure in forgiveness.

But what is this thing called forgiveness? Really? Forgiveness is a quiet miracle. It is done alone. When we pardon, we give up our resentment toward a perceived offender in the silence of our heart and mind. No one can record our miracle on videotape. Our decision is private and invisible, a sincere whisper heard deep in our spirit.

Nothing clutters a life, or the life of a nation, more than the three R's: resentment, remorse, and recrimination. These three emotional responses to life are based in anger, guilt, and hostility. When held in the mind and in the heart, they occupy a fearsome amount of space, coloring our perception of reality to an alarmingly large degree. They block our potential. They drain our life of any chance for joy and peace.

Enter the great non-negotiable Law of Forgiveness—the one and only key that opens the lock of hostility. Forgiveness of others and forgiveness of ourselves. We all have the power to do this here, now.

Forgiveness frees us from the perpetual self-punishment that the decision to hate demands. Forgiveness allows us to neutralize the toxic emotional investment that keeps us in shackles. Our decision to forgive allows us freedom. It is the only key on the ring that unlocks the shackles of grudge and guilt.

Forgiveness. Understand the depth of what this law is asking of us. We forgive not to let the other person off the hook. No. We forgive to let ourselves off the hook. And magically, almost mystically, we receive a new life, a healed life.

The consequences of not forgiving are high. The person who hates by constantly carrying a toxic attitude of resentment into his or her relationships, who goes through life spreading animosity, has chosen a distorted and darkened lens with which to view life. Hate is the death of wellness. The inevitable results include marriages that lack trust, jobs that create situations of constant friction and interpersonal relations filled with toxicity.

Life is filtered through our perceptions, shaded with whatever colors we choose. Choose the color of hate and the penalty is a life experience filled with acid rancor, deep disappointment, and self-pitying paranoia. We fear what others may do, or fail to do, to us and for us. Our response: hate. Through anger, through attack, through defense, we feel we find a certain, though unstable, sense of safety.

This behavior is everywhere. Recently, I was deeply saddened to hear that some young Jewish friends had been chased by two boys wielding wooden sticks. Our friends were targets of religious hatred perpetrated by children too young to really understand the meaning of their actions. One can only assume that the two young boys learned this hatred from their parents.

As much as I wanted to encourage our friends to fight back, I recognized that this would be a decision to hate. The decision to hate only perpetuates the problem. Only forgiveness can conquer the hatred.

Marilyn was recovering from treatments for ovarian cancer. Her parents wanted to visit, an event that invariably left Marilyn ill at ease. Marilyn and her mother made noble efforts to get along with each other but they seldom succeeded fully. Old behaviors of attack and defense eventually came to the surface. Child care, cooking, homemaking, religion—it was all fodder for conflict. Her mother wanted a more conservative daughter. Marilyn wanted a more enlightened mother.

"It was driving me crazy," said Marilyn.

"During her last visit, I was ready to throw her out. But then it occurred to me, God isn't looking at my mother and thinking, 'Mildred is such a bitch.' How could I pretend to want to get along with my mother if I was so consumed by judging her errors? I needed to practice forgiveness, to work on acceptance and get off my fixation with approval.

"So I said to myself, 'I'll try this for an afternoon. I will put my energy into accepting her, no matter what.'" The experiment was life-changing. From that moment on, the relationship started to shift. "As I silently forgave her and became more accepting, she became more accepting of me. We're a long way from best buddies," conceded Marilyn, "but there is a growing bond between us."

I am a student of forgiveness, not a master. We recently purchased a new home. In the course of a couple of visits that took place after we signed the offer, we learned of several major problems that had not been disclosed during inspection: the basement filled with water when it rained, and water seeping through the leaky roof had damaged the rafters.

I responded in all the wrong ways. My ego roared. My emotions surged. I felt I had been lied to. I believed people were trying to cheat me. I became determined to "get even." So I hired an attorney: I'd threaten to sue and drive the seller and the agent to the bargaining table.

A settlement was reached. But I found myself unable to give up the anger. I knew what I should do: forgive. I was unable to do it.

The Law of Forgiveness is a tough taskmaster. It forces us to examine our motives. It requires us to look deep within. The work of forgiveness demands that we give up the need to always be right. That is a big request.

The Law of Forgiveness can be misunderstood. It is not asking us to betray our deepest beliefs or disregard our principles. We need not compromise our personal integrity by failing to stand up for what we hold to be true. The law does not imply that we are to live our lives trying to please everyone at the risk of being untrue to ourselves.

However, the law does ask us to become keenly aware of how often we engage in verbal and emotional combat that has less to do with higher principles and personal integrity than it does with our perceptions of being right.

In the larger scheme of my life, how important is it, really, that I get to be "right" in a real-estate transaction? And once a settlement has been agreed to, how important is it that I keep rehashing the experience?

The Law of Forgiveness demands that I come to a very important realization: in these matters, it is not my spirit that demands to be right, it is my frail ego.

In fact, it is probably my ego that has backed me into this situation in the first place. And my ego is not the most reliable source of guidance in getting me out of the situation.

Realize that this law and its demands are as true of marriages as of real-estate transactions. Forgiveness is for the workplace and for parenting, for young and old, for black and white. Forgiveness applies to everything, to everyone, all the time. This is what is meant by life being lived most abundantly as an adventure in forgiveness.

Nothing contaminates the life of wellness more than resentment, remorse, and recrimination. These states of heart and mind do more to stand in the way of our wellness than virtually any other dynamic.

IF THE DAILY PRACTICE of the Law of Forgiveness is the only way out, what does this law look like in action?

I know from vivid personal experience. I can trace the absolute turning point in my own illness directly to the work of forgiveness. Weak, emaciated, lying at home in constant pain, I was going downhill rapidly by all physical measurements. Doctors, family, even my own mind—all believed I was about to die.

Yet something kept driving me. I would place phone calls to organizations all over the country, seeking others who had gone through a similar situation and lived. I wanted to learn from their experience.

I kept hearing people talk about forgiveness. "You need to forgive," said a woman in Boise, Idaho. A man from Tennessee put it plainly: "The difference is forgiveness."

My first reaction was "I probably don't have many issues of forgiveness to deal with. Forgiveness isn't my problem."

I was wrong. Forgiveness *was* my issue. My critical attitude was first. Why did I look at a situation and always pick out what was wrong? I'd do it constantly. People were my favorite target. I would make a quick study of someone and actively seek out his Achilles' heel. "What's wrong with him?" I'd think. It was all an effort to put someone else down in order to build myself up. Distorted thinking, bereft of charity and compassion.

The worst example was my behavior at work. When a new controller was brought in, and I suddenly had to seek approval for all our division's expense budgets through this new "intruder," I saw the whole setup as a huge threat to my position. So, without really making a conscious decision, I began to attack. I became critical of the controller's plans. I tried to undermine his work. I threw stones at his policies. I became critical of him personally.

My criticism led to condemnation. I set myself up as judge and jury. If I was superior, then I was right. In fact, I always had to be right. Therefore, the new controller was, by definition, wrong. I condemned him and then went about proving it to others.

As I look back, I see that it was only three months between the time the new controller came on board and the onset of my cancer diagnosis. I believe there was a link between my toxic behavior and the onset of my illness.

What I didn't count on was a counterattack. The new controller fought back, pointing out my failures to institute more effective financial controls. He was equally skilled at finding a person's weak point. And the battle between the two of us became a company-wide problem that began to drag everyone down.

I am saddened and mortified about how it came to a head. We were in a meeting with three other division heads and the CEO. My adversary the controller passed around a budget update. Trying to be flippant, I took my copy of the document, threw it across the table, and proclaimed, "These numbers are a crock of ——." The report hit the CEO's coffee cup, the contents of which spilled into his lap.

He jumped up, glared at me, pointed a finger, and said, "Get the hell out of here." I went back to my office, then headed to my car. I began to see how absolutely ludicrous my behavior had been.

That kind of behavior consumes vast amounts of emotional energy. It produces a negative and contrary spirit that is toxic to us and to others. I had my entire sense of worth invested in always being right. I suppose it was an issue of perception. I was so concerned with what other people thought of me that I never considered I might be wrong. I needed everyone to know that I was right and to acknowledge it.

But the story takes an even more bizarre twist. Within thirty days of my diagnosis of lung cancer, my adversary the controller was diagnosed with prostate cancer. Now, I have had medical authorities tell me that he probably had been carrying the cancer for years and it had just then been discovered, as had mine. But my intuition tells me that our toxic battle contributed to the onset of both illnesses.

I underwent surgery that removed a lung. But surgery was impossible for my nemesis the controller. The disease had already spread. As the weeks passed, both of us grew progressively worse.

Four months later, a second surgery confirmed that the cancer had spread from my lung through the lymph system. The following day the surgeon made a statement that is indelibly etched in my mind. "Greg," he said, "the tiger is out of the cage. Your cancer has come roaring back. I'd give you about thirty days to live."

It was at that moment that I began my journey in search of wellness. Lying in bed, at home, I continued to deteriorate physically. But I made those phone calls in search of survivors and I kept hearing "forgive."

One morning I awoke and realized that I did have a monumental task of forgiveness ahead of me. I felt a deep conviction that this was the thing for me to do. From my sickbed I began the solitary work of forgiveness. I believe that this was the precise turning point in my illness.

The Law of Forgiveness carries with it the idea of process. That is, there are actions and conscious decisions that are integral to the forgiveness phenomenon. Any number of legitimate ways to proceed exist, but they each share this idea of helping us release resentment, express negative feelings, and let go of past wrongs, both real and imagined. Once the idea of process has been grasped, it only needs to be applied with consistency and sincerity to bring immediate results.

The essence of the various processes is quite simple: become aware of the person toward whom we feel hostility, express active release from that hostility, and picture good things happening to him or her.

In the privacy of my bedroom, I made a sign on a sheet of paper. It read:

NAME

RELEASE

AFFIRM

With that sign propped at my bedside, I started a list of the people in my life. I put my wife first. I closed my eyes, relaxed, and created a clear picture of her in my mind. Then, from my heart, I imagined myself saying to her, "I forgive you. I totally and completely forgive you for every perceived wrong you have done—and for anything you have left undone." And I would pause, allowing ample time to remember and release specific instances. I wouldn't dwell on the specifics. I would just recall them and release them, recognizing that it was I, not my wife, who was really being let off the hook.

I would end the work with each person by pictur-
ing something good happening to him or her. I knew
that my wife wanted and needed to receive continual
reassurance of my love for her. I pictured her receiving
that. I knew that another person with whom I'd had a
falling-out wanted a new sports car. I imagined him
happily driving down the freeway in his red Porsche.
The point is, part of the process I used was to actively
see something good happening to the person I was forgiving.

This was not always a smooth experience. It became fascinating for me to watch my own resistance.
It was relatively easy to express forgiveness and mean it.
To actively release the hurt was more challenging, but
repeating the release three or four times typically helped
me make the emotional and spiritual shift that was required. Many times I would say, "God, you take this.
I cannot handle it anymore."

The third element of the process was the real test for
me. It was difficult to envision good things happening to
many of the people I wanted and needed to forgive. But
I was sincerely committed to the process. I did not have
an expectation of ease. I would see this through.

I discovered I was intensely angry with my father.
He never was able to express his love. In fact, his approach to child raising was to emotionally put down
and never, not once, build up. I found it very difficult
to totally release my perceptions of being wronged. And
I found it next to impossible to imagine, with sincerity,

something good happening to him. I spent nearly two days just on the work of forgiving my father. Tough stuff.

The work on forgiving my father taught me an important lesson. His actions resulted from huge hurts of his own. They had nothing to do with me. The inability to express love was a direct reflection of his own upbringing. I shifted my perspective from blaming him for all that was missing to understanding how I may also have contributed to the situation. I was rebellious. I did not obey. I was sarcastic. Perhaps the only way to reach me was through put-downs.

This insight extended to other relationships. As I would forgive and release, I still might not approve of the way a person handled a particular situation. But after completing the process of forgiveness, I could generally *understand* the situation better and begin to see my own part in it.

Down the list I went. Name people; forgive and release them; affirm them. Many times I went back to names, especially those where the memories created feelings of unease. And I offered my forgiveness with deep sincerity.

Sometimes forgiveness requires work above and beyond the call of duty. This was the case with the controller. I had spent hours forgiving and releasing and trying to imagine great things happening to him. About noon of the fourth straight day of forgiveness, I came out of the bedroom for lunch. It was then I realized that my work with him needed to take on a more personal touch. I needed to visit him and express my apologies.

This was not easy. I made a call to the office and found that he was at home, and not doing well. I phoned and his wife answered. Her voice immediately telegraphed surprise and shock to be talking to me; she knew full well the battle that raged between her husband and me.

I said, "I want to come out and visit, this afternoon. When would be a good time?"

She said she'd have to check. "I'll hang on," I replied. The time was set.

When was the last time your heart felt like it would pound right out of your chest? My emotions went on overdrive. On the way to his house, I wanted to turn back. My steps in making the short walk between the curb and his front door were some of the most difficult I have ever taken. The whole time, my heart was in my throat. But I pressed on. I felt that my life hinged on this sincere effort at forgiveness.

What do you say to someone whom you have previously considered an enemy? How do you communicate your changed feelings? Are words ever adequate to make up for the emotional havoc one has caused?

I was greeted and led into the bedroom, where my adversary was propped up in his bed with pillows. And with my heart pounding, adrenaline rushing, voice shaking, I barely managed to stutter out a few words to this effect:

"I have come to say I am sorry." A long pause to gather some composure. My voice still breaking, I continued:

"I deeply regret the hurt I have caused you." Another pause. I remember my right hand and arm were shaking, out of my control. I tried to steady them with my left hand.

In a whisper I finished: "I want you to know I wish you only the very best."

Those words were imperfect, to be sure. They were delivered in a voice that was gripped with fear. But they came from my heart, sincere in every aspect.

They must have been effective. Because my adversary struggled to sit up, swung his feet over the edge of the bed, and motioned me to come and sit by his side.

"Greg," he said, "I am the one who needs to say I'm sorry. I'm old enough to be your father. Yet I treated you like the outcast son. Please forgive me."

His wife was crying. She knelt on the floor and the three of us embraced. We all cried.

Finally, it was my old adversary who found the strength to mutter a prayer: "Dear God, forgive us all."

We said brief good-byes and I left.

As I started the car back toward home, I took a deep breath and said out loud, "Whew!" A weight was being lifted. I could feel it, sense it, was part of it: the clouds that had been tormenting me were beginning to part.

The day seemed brighter. Was it the sun, or was it this catharsis that had just taken place?

My posture changed. I went from being hunched over to sitting erect in the seat. I held my head more upright. The tension in my shoulders lessened dramatically. The wrinkles on my forehead melted away. I relaxed. The pain was gone. The quivering hand was steady. A smile came across my face.

"I'm free!" I whispered. "I'm free," I repeated, this time louder. In a crescendo I exclaimed, "I'm free! I'm free! I'm free!" I shouted it: "I'm free!"

Tears gushed down my cheeks in torrents. My vision became blurred. I quickly pulled off onto a side street, parked the car, and wept, out of control, for a long, long time.

I remember the eyes of a lad who came to the window. I wonder how long he had been watching me. "Hey, mister," he said, "you need help?"

"No, no. I'm fine." And I made my way home.

RELEASE. SET FREE. I look back to my week of the sincere work of forgiveness and realize this was the absolute turning point in my physical healing. From that point in time, I began to gain back lost weight, manage pain more readily, and hold more positive thoughts about my future.

Do I believe there was a link between this deeply spiritual work and my physical improvement? Absolutely. I believe that practicing the Law of Forgiveness changes us biochemically. And in the process, the body is released toward its optimum wellness potential.

I know that my doctor and scientist friends get very uncomfortable when I share these beliefs. But it seems we can all agree on this: life quality soars when we sincerely practice the Law of Forgiveness. And this just may be an important determinant in releasing the body's self-healing potential.

Life can indeed be lived most abundantly as an adventure in forgiveness. Forgive. Set yourself free.

20

The Law of
Gratitude

Affirm the good things.

Millions of dollars have been wasted on health and life improvement programs that couldn't possibly work, no matter how brilliant or clever. Or how determined the participants.

Many people just assume that the latest expensive exercise contraption has all the answers to life's problems. Not so.

Remember the Law of Unity: this all works together—body, mind, and spirit. Nudge the body all you want. But until habits of the mind and spirit change, we'll never know wellness.

What is the worst spiritual habit, the one that causes disappointment, conflict, loss, and dis-ease of every kind? I've heard people speculate with answers that range from laziness to blasphemy against God. Some have said procrastination. Others thought it to be criticism. All good choices.

But the absolute worst habit is ingratitude. Yes, ingratitude—the lack of thankfulness and appreciation, our poor return for blessings and kindness received.

A woman came early to a seminar in Greenwich, Connecticut, and insisted on seeing me. After a few words, it became apparent she had become an emotional, spiritual, and physical wreck through dwelling on her problems. She complained about a missed cancer diagnosis, the terror of treatments, mistreatment by doctors, and abandonment by family.

Finally, I couldn't take it anymore. I said, "Now that you have told me all that is wrong with you, tell me something that is right with you."

Almost in anger the woman declared there was nothing right with her. She was shocked that I persisted. "There are many things right," I began. "You're able to walk, talk, eat, breathe, see, hear, taste, smell. You're not bedridden. You're not helpless. You have some degree of health or you wouldn't be here tonight."

I advised her, "Listen carefully this evening. Then go home and for the next three weeks concentrate on what is right in your life. Refuse to speak of your ills. And thank God each and every waking hour for your health, your blessings, and your life." As she left, I was determined to do my best to reach her that night.

When I think about the blessings in my life, I am touched by a letter I recently received from a friend who is in prison on tax-evasion charges. It's one of the most powerful letters I have ever received. In it my friend chastises me for complaining—for being bogged down with ingratitude.

"You're free—I wish I could say that. You're in

debt—I am too. I have to pay the government $165,000 per month for 3 years. You're in sunny California. Last night the actual temperature here was 35 degrees below zero and we have three feet of snow. You're doing what you love to do. I'm an orderly and clean toilets every morning. (But I'm the best damn orderly they've ever had around this place!)"

That letter was the proverbial kick in the pants I needed. I read it again and again. It became crystal clear to me that I was looking at life through the eyes of ingratitude. I needed to change, to see a new me.

I opened to a new page in my wellness journal and wrote a heading, "I am grateful for:" Under this I divided the page into three columns: "People," "Places," and "Things." I became inspired. My pen was a whirl-wind as I wrote: wife, daughter, love, health, life, home, car, books, ideas, opportunities—a long list of all that I was thankful for.

What resulted was a "new look" at myself through the lens of gratitude. I determined that I would hold that image in my consciousness. It would be the picture I would continuously flash on the screen of my mind. Gratitude would become the new me!

JOHN ROBERT MCFARLAND, in his excellent book *Now That I Have Cancer, I Am Whole,* gives us a pene-trating insight into gratitude-based thinking:

I'm so grateful I never have bad days. I have nause-
ated days and frightened days. Tired days and hurt-
ing days. Long days and short days. Silent days and
alone days. Mouth-sore days and swollen-hand
days. Bald days and diarrhea days. Rainy days and
sunny days. Cold days and warm days. But no bad
days. I'm so grateful.

McFarland is teaching us that one simple concept
can get us through the most difficult times. It's the Law
of Gratitude. It may be the most important part of the
wellness journey.

Every time you have a negative thought, counter
it with a thought of gratitude. Problems, negativity, even
dis-ease are transformed by the sincere application of
this dynamic law.

Imagine my friend, in prison, on the receiving end
of my letter, which was filled with miserable talk. He's
the one who had reason for complaint. Where was my
gratitude? After an exchange of letters, we talked on the
phone. I said, "Thank you for opening my eyes. God
has given me so many opportunities to help others.
Thank you for helping me get the proper perspective."
I expressed my thanks.

The Law of Gratitude requires us to express appreciation in more ways than words. My whole demeanor
started to change. I resolved to back my words with actions. My posture, my walk, even my facial expressions

and gestures took on a whole new appearance. I asked myself, "If I feel grateful, how can I act grateful?" Then I began immediately to respond to those thoughts.

I put the Law of Gratitude to a test by expressing my appreciation to my wife for her love and support. I thanked her for always starting our days with a hug and a kiss. I said thanks for changing the way we cook so I could shift toward a more vegetarian diet. My expressions were of true gratitude, not flattery. The difference? One is sincere, the other insincere. Dale Carnegie made the distinction succinctly: "One comes from the heart out; the other from the teeth out."

I continued this work of gratitude in all the key areas of my life—my health, my career, my finances, my other important relationships, and my spiritual work. Some of the entries in my gratitude list: my health, being cancer-free, the ability to walk, my renewed strength. As I thought of my career I wrote that I was grateful for "the ability to help people, developing good listening skills, the ability to speak in front of a group, the opportunity to write about what is important to me."

And I expressed my deep gratitude to God, recognizing God as the source of all that is good, the only one capable of giving the gift of another day.

The more I contemplated my blessings, the more I felt a sweeping change in my emotional and spiritual outlook. What was happening? I was taking cognitive charge of my expression of gratitude. It was changing my entire being.

The Law of Gratitude carries with it the potential for wellness miracles. The feeling of gratitude—this emotional and spiritual happy, abundant, free attitude—makes things right. It changes you, and me, deep within. Then, and only then, does it change our world.

The woman from Greenwich whom I challenged wrote to me some months after my admonishment: "It's been a year now since my last treatment. I just came through my checkup with flying colors. You were right. There's a lot to be grateful for."

It's not that I was right, it's that she was right. She was right when she started to focus on being grateful.

The wellness path requires us to embrace a proactive expression of sincere gratitude. Try it for a week, a day, an hour. Observe the results. You will be amazed at the changes in yourself, your health, your relationships, your career—your entire life.

Affirm the good things in your life and watch them expand. It's the non-negotiable, irrevocable Law of Gratitude.

21

The Law of
Personal Peace

Without inner peace, it is impossible
to have world peace.

—*The Dalai Lama*

One of the most important and lofty goals of the wellness journey is to attain peace—inner peace, "the peace that passes all understanding."

But one of our early discoveries as we begin the wellness journey is how much we are at war with ourselves. We are angry over our mistakes, we resent our weaknesses, we resist fulfilling our highest aspirations. We want wellness in all areas of life but we don't like the price.

Resolution of these conflicts resides in understanding and practicing the non-negotiable Law of Personal Peace.

Four of my close friends have gathered with me on our deck. We are considering the subject of satisfaction. "There simply has to be more to life than getting up, going to work, coming home, and going to bed," my friend Bud is saying. "I've tried every self-help book ever written. I have so many doubts and questions. Frankly, I'm discouraged."

"I'm with you," says Manny. "I'm terrified of getting cancer again. I know I need to make changes in my life, but look at all my responsibilities. I can't walk away from my business. I gotta figure out how to put up with it—I gotta make it happen."

"Satisfaction?" says Chester wistfully. "I could probably count on one hand the number of times I've felt satisfied."

Joe, the senior of the group, shakes his head and says, "I wouldn't know satisfaction if it came up and slapped me in the face. What do you mean by satisfaction anyway?"

These four people are all men of accomplishment. They have received honors in their work, they volunteer in positions of service in their community, and they are active in their spiritual quests. Yet not one could say he consistently knew and experienced satisfaction. It's a scene repeated in countless lives around this planet.

The wellness journey holds out the high promise of inner peace. To live knowing this powerful yet subtle quality is to be so attuned with the spiritual power of compassion and love as to be counted among those closest to living to their Divine potential. But what is this personal peace? And how can we find it?

Personal peace is that inner, ethereal sense of emotional and spiritual well-being, the deep tranquility that comes when we can disconnect from disquieting or threatening thoughts.

Subjective, but very real, personal peace is the grounded and connected feeling when we let go of worry, pain, stress, and fear and become mindful of life's myriad wonders.

Personal peace is the knowledge that all is well, an understanding that God has everything under control, even when our world may seem ready to explode. It comes when we mentally, emotionally, spiritually, and sometimes physically disengage ourselves from painful, dis-ease-producing entanglements with another person, with conflicts, or with our responsibilities.

Personal peace becomes a reality when we shift our focus from problems we cannot solve to a higher vision of hopefulness. We transcend. In this shift we allow sorrow and worry to fall away. The bliss that remains is peace.

My mother was a world-champion worrier. She would constantly make herself upset by ruminating over the "what ifs" of life. What if the car runs out of gas. What if there's not enough money? What if my children are in an accident. What if we get sick and end up in the hospital. What if, what if, what if. Her worries kept her awake as she fought chronic insomnia. No matter what glorious event was happening in her life, it was always tainted by her worries. To her, life was mostly fearful, the future always foreboding. For her there were few moments of personal peace.

Choosing to focus on regrets of the past can also rob us of personal peace. These are the "if onlys" — if only I had better parents, then my life would have turned out happy. If only I took better care of myself, then I wouldn't be sick. If only I lived in a different part of the country. If only, if only, if only. If you want to be certain of never knowing personal peace, start reciting the if onlys.

If we intend to successfully travel the highway of wellness and reach the destination of personal peace, we're going to have to dismantle some of these personal roadblocks; fear of the future and regret over the past are only the primary ones. The full wellness journey means we'll also have to move past the potholes of envy, the detour signs of impatience, the dead ends of willfulness, and the ice-covered bridges of rigidity. But travel we must. The wellness journey is not taken in a parked car.

The way of peace? Through prayerful meditation, a forgotten and misunderstood discipline. Prayerful meditation is an excellent way to develop increased awareness in all areas of life. But it is essential in attaining and sustaining personal peace.

When we are caught up in worry or attack or defense, we are effectively absent without leave from our potential for wellness. The well person isn't at home. For example, we may be driving, become enraged over the traffic, and entirely miss the beautiful sunset. Instead, we focus on inner scenes of worry and fear.

Prayerful meditation helps us shift our attention to the present moment and to control of our mind and spirit. It brings us back home. Now we can let go of our cares and become open and aware of the divine presence. I know of no other effective way to attain personal peace.

Prayerful meditation has become an extremely important part of my life. I set aside a time each day for this activity. And when I am home, I have a special place where I meditate. I have a favorite rocking chair in my home office. Next to the chair is a table with an old beat-up brass lamp sitting on it. I also have my favorite books there, and a few special personal remembrances: a framed note from Norman Vincent Peale, pictures of my family. This is my "nest." When I close the door and sit in this chair, I become automatically attuned to the experience of peace, of the divine presence.

I meditate once a day for approximately twenty minutes. I'll increase the frequency or the duration if I am particularly harried. The techniques I use are simple and basic; anyone can do them. Through mindful awareness, I allow my mind to relax. I consciously let go of negative emotions. And then I connect with God, becoming aware of the loving presence that suffuses all of life. Many times I'll silently repeat the word *peace*.

This experience almost always allows me to find the peace I seek. It's a point of control, a way to naturally tranquilize my tensions and to be in harmony with our world.

It's my way of implementing the Law of Personal Peace. Other ways exist, to be sure. But all have the common bond of a conscious seeking to calm the mind, to center the spirit, to know personal peace.

I've been privileged to teach wellness in many places, and I always attempt to include a special section on personal peace. One of the most widely accepted ideas of personal peace ties its attainment to passivity and relaxation. I suppose it's because we associate meditation with the ideas of becoming relaxed and passive.

One woman in Montreal said, "I thought personal peace meant a state of low energy and rest, a time when I avoid any exertion." A young man from England remarked, "Personal peace? I thought I'd need to spend all my time in quiet meditation."

In fact, the opposite is true. A deep sense of personal peace brings with it enormous energy. It is a body/mind/spirit state from which our highest, most effective actions flow. Personal peace creates a state of being that provides maximum energy for whatever we choose to do. And that energy is focused and effective because it comes from a peaceful center.

At times progress on the journey is measured by inches instead of miles. We struggle. The serenity is gone. We find nothing for which we are grateful. Our ability to give and receive love in mutually enhancing and empowering ways seems lost. We're angry or depressed. Guilt may haunt us. We feel overly responsible for others. We want to give, we attempt to help, we try to love. But our travels seem to lead us down one blind alley after another. The peace we seek eludes us.

Even day-to-day living can thwart personal peace. Driving a car can become a matter of intense competition, even hostility. Arguments over defective appliances, utility bills, and bank statement errors are commonplace. Domestic quarrels, even between loving and compassionate couples, are inevitable.

All this takes enormous effort. The inner conflicts drain our resources. Peace is lost. We become so immersed in resolving this inner warfare that we have little energy to do anything more in the world than get by. And there are moments when even getting by is difficult.

The problem is not that we lack energy, even though we may feel tired and weary. We do have the energy. The problem is that it's fragmented. We clearly need to find a firm base for our wellness. The Law of Personal Peace is that base.

So we declare an inner truce. We momentarily allow ourselves to withdraw from the raging battle. We take time for "the quiets." We become aware of our battles and exhaustion.

This awareness puts us at a critical crossroads. One path leads back to the battle. The other way leads to detachment, to release and to personal peace.

Hopefully, we often choose to detach. We practice prayerful meditation. As a result, we gain perspective.

We realize our inner conflicts are not eternal. But we must not remain detached from our duty to act. The energy that once fueled our raging internal battle now can be used for creative living. With practice, we become focused and serene. Our emotional and spiritual energy then skyrockets. And we stand ready, recharged, renewed for service to our world.

Personal peace generates energy. Our increase in effective physical, emotional, and spiritual energy is the result of our discovery of inner peace. And its more effective use means that we are less likely to waste our precious resources on worry, regret, blame, and indecision. This is a giant step toward wellness on the highest spiritual level.

As we progress along the wellness path, the law of Personal Peace helps us become true peacemakers, not in the usual sense of composing the quarrels of other people or nations. But instead, we become peacemakers when we bring about serenity in our own souls. Then we are filled with a positive power, a spirit that energizes. And as that energy is used for good, it increases. It will meet all our needs, and flow to help others.

I believe personal peace is the vibrant energy that can heal the world, that can make peace between nations a reality. Peace certainly cannot be brought about by superficial negotiations, temporary agreements, or signatures on pieces of paper. Since the beginning of recorded history, tens of thousands of peace treaties have been signed but have not been able to sustain peace. Clearly the lesson is to look deeper, to seek resolution of conflict personally from the inside out. I believe personal peace and personal peace alone can bring lasting harmony in the world.

Simple acts, really, are the things that change our lives and our world. The conscious pursuit of peace is one of those. If you're serious about your wellness journey, become a peacemaker. Release. Renew. Recommit. Make friends early with the non-negotiable Law of Personal Peace.

The Greatest Law

22

The Law of
Unconditional Loving

. . . and the greatest of these is love.

—*Saint Paul*

We are each given but one life. Once and only once can we live it.

Each life contains no promises. Only possibilities. It is the great privilege of each person to pursue his or her highest potential. This pursuit, undertaken with sincerity, is the true wellness journey.

What then is the ultimate object of this pursuit, the goal that transcends all others, that surpasses health, wealth, and power? I believe it to be the consistent practice of the Law of Unconditional Loving.

Medicine tells us that health is the greatest goal. But health is not the greatest thing in life. Greatness exists in places where health is absent. In fact, good health may lull us into complacency and lessen our interest in attaining the greatest goal.

Academicians tell us that the wise use of knowledge is the highest order of living. Learning, wisdom—these are the supreme objects to covet. But wisdom does not capture the high ground. Many who claim wisdom fail the test of true greatness. A false sense of wisdom may blind us to the highest pursuit.

Politicians say the quest for liberty is our supreme calling. Freedom, the pursuit of happiness—these are what our hearts yearn for most. But all the freedom in the world will not take the place of the benefits of the ultimate quest. The greatest goal is able to thrive in slavery as well as freedom.

Social and political scientists tell us to see good works as the supreme accomplishment. Helping others, service without regard for self—these are the goal. Yet all the good works may simply leave us tired, our true potential unfulfilled. Good works often result from the pursuit of the highest goal, but they are not the goal.

Capitalists say economic freedom is our highest calling. If we could just implement the market system worldwide, all the other benefits of modern society would be possible. But even a cursory examination shows the capitalists' ideas to be wanting. Supreme happiness does not equate with economic wealth. The greatest attainment is possible for both the rich and the poor.

Religion tells us that the greatest thing to possess is faith. Faith in God, in ourselves, in our fellow humans. This assurance, trust, and belief in our connection with the Ultimate is what we are after, say the clerics. Sadly, the pursuit of faith has a checkered history that is long on wars and oppression, short on peace and personal compassion. In the name of faith, atrocities have been committed on large segments of society. Faith is not the supreme attainment.

Medicine, academia, politics, social philosophy, capitalism, even religion all consistently miss the mark. If we base our lives on their precepts, we, too, will miss the mark of our highest calling.

The greatest pursuit is not good health, unsurpassed wisdom, economic surplus, political freedom, or even faith that can move mountains.

It is the daily practice of the greatest of the nonnegotiable laws of wellness, the Law of Unconditional Loving.

Unconditional, nonjudgmental loving. This is our aim, life's single highest and most rewarding pursuit.

I like the word *loving* better than *love* because it tends to communicate the action required to make love real.

The ideal of unconditional loving has been pursued through the centuries, sometimes with brief success, mostly without. Some people claim that it is unattainable, outside the reach of human capability. Others acknowledge the potential of unconditional loving but fail to personalize its mandate.

Yet living the message of unconditional loving is very possible indeed. This greatest non-negotiable law can be our unfailing guiding light if we will ask but one question: What is the loving thing to do?

Asked consistently and responded to with courage, this one question can transform a life, save a marriage, shape a child, reignite a career, even change the world. *What is the loving thing to do?*

ALL SUCCESS, all well-being, all self-improvement has its basis in an unfathomable spirit that sustains us even when we may be least aware of it. That spirit is love.

The law's question—What is the loving thing to do?—is another way of asking, What is God's way of doing this? In the answer to this question we find supernatural power for living.

Some people do not believe there is a God. I do. But I realize that when people think about God, we very often have vastly different ideas. I've found it most meaningful to think of God as the Ultimate Source, creator of all, giver of life, always present in every corner of creation, in every moment of time.

I also believe that as human beings, we cannot attain God's perfection. But I've also observed that to the degree to which we align ourselves with the principles found in the Laws of Wellness, God's potential will then be released within and through us, enabling us to come closer to our Divine Design.

The highest expression of Divine Design is applied love found in loving relationships between people. Not the erotic love we see on television and in the movies but love rooted in a decision to serve. It is a dynamic state of consciousness, a giving, creative flow, and a harmony. It's an acceptance of the human condition as perfectly imperfect. And it is a choice to love without regard to any conditions; no "ifs" are allowed in this, the greatest of the laws.

I have seen cancer respond to the decision to love, and have personally experienced such a response as well. After a sincere and thorough effort at forgiveness, I made a decision to love, as best I could, without any condition. Suddenly the cancer and a thirty-days-to-live prognosis appeared in a totally different light.

My decision to practice the Law of Unconditional Loving meant I could love people who only weeks before had seemed unlovable, even pathetic. My aim was not to reduce my suffering or postpone my imminent death. Rather, it was to live life now, to make the most of the moment. Only unconditional loving could fulfill those objectives.

I didn't have to get in touch with my anger, my fear, or my despair. I'd discovered those emotions already. But there was little value in knowing what I was feeling unless I could transcend the feelings. And I found my ability to transcend rooted in love.

Despite the physical pain, despite my deep fears, despite the fact that my spiritual foundations had crumbled, I now came to understand that it was my sole job to love. In that discovery were the seeds of wellness on the highest level I had ever known.

When I became completely willing to allow God's love to pour through me, my life changed. I figured that as long as I was breathing I was here to be a channel for God's love. God works through people. I was a person. God could work through *me!* It was in this very decision that I discovered the basis for massive positive change.

I've come to believe there is nothing in this world as important as unconditional loving. To allow the gradual and ever-increasing release of that love is my most important task. No higher call exists. No greater satisfaction awaits.

I practice what I call a "Daily Act of Loving." At least once a day, typically just before lunch, I make it a discipline to reach out in unconditional love to another person. The value and results of this practice have changed my life. That one simple decision to act with unconditional love affects every decision, every relationship. It greatly improves the quality and the effectiveness of my entire day, including the restfulness of my sleep. I believe my Daily Act of Loving gives me the strength to handle the difficult challenges of life. And I commend to you the simple practice of extending unconditional love to another person at least once a day, every day, for the rest of your life. You'll heal your world in delightful and surprising ways.

Yet it is important to understand that love's power can be trivialized. "Love heals" has been a popular notion for centuries. It has enjoyed a recent resurgence that has had an unfortunate side effect. Many people who do not get well, in the sense of a clinical cure, are made to feel guilty that they were not able to care enough or demonstrate ample enough compassion to effect healing. For them, love does not heal. Love is a cruel master.

This "guilt-tripping," this illusion that we have total control, misses the point entirely. It damages the individual and it relegates unconditional loving to a technique, a modality in health and healing. Love is much more than a prescription. There is no formula that universally links spiritual perfection and clinical cures. Those who make such claims are misguided.

Rather, love transforms suffering—a crucial distinction. That transformation may include a clinical cure; it may not. Cure is not the standard for judging. For even the process of death is transformed by unconditional loving. We can leave the world filled with joyful memories, an example of how to love. That's healing of the highest order. And death cannot be counted, then, as failure.

Love creates. The Law of Unconditional Loving calls for a fundamental shift in our conceptual framework of reality itself! The law's power extends far beyond our personal wellness or our individual lives. By our response of love, we become co-creators of a world with endless possibilities.

By our words, thoughts, actions, and prayers, we co-create our life. Our inner processes do indeed affect our physical world. We influence events, relationships, opportunities, financial opportunities. . . . We create.

The most powerful, beneficial form of creation is unconditional loving. It offers a way to think, to be, to experience life. When a spirit becomes saturated with unconditional love, a new reality is created no matter what the circumstance.

Illness is not the only path to this realization. Every person's life has in it a crisis point. Unconditional loving applied to the crisis always—yes, always—improves the circumstances. The conditions may not change so much as our response to them. And in that change lies all the difference.

Seeing life through the lens of unconditional loving frees us from the constraints of the "ordinary." No longer are we locked into using outdated, outmoded, toxic, and questionably effective solutions to problems. The automatic response of attack-and-defend can be dropped. And in its place, a decision to be a channel for unconditional goodwill and love can give us new and effective resolution. A Daily Act of Loving starts this whole miracle.

Clearly, the ordinary thinking of traditional solutions, be it medical thinking, political thinking, or religious thinking, is no longer expansive enough to embrace solutions to the problems of this world.

The Law of Unconditional Loving holds the best, the only, answer.

The Law of Unconditional Loving is actually spirituality in motion. Even if we have difficulty in accept-

ing the existence of God or of some form of divine intel-
ligence, we can demonstrate and accept for ourselves
the idea that the extension of love to another person can
change two lives: the life that receives the love and the
life that does the loving.

What does this tell us? What instruction does this
give us? How then do we live our lives? At a minimum,
it suggests that to live unconsciously, to live unaware of
how we are thinking, feeling, loving, and thus creating,
is a real threat to our health and greater well-being.
Learning to live and love consciously, developing the
skills of awareness and insight, releases a person from
having to feel victimized or controlled by life's challenges. Love is personal power. Loving transforms ordinary human consciousness into a force that changes our
very world.

Think of a person you know who is dedicated to
truly loving. The presence of such a person is unmistak-
able. She or he resonates with a spirit and communicates an energy that says, "People are welcome and safe
here." Love knocks down all the usual barriers.

This is love at its best: an attitude of nonjudgmen-
talism, an acceptance for all of life. People with spirits
dedicated to loving are awakened to the truth that they
are co-creators with God.

Practicing the Law of Unconditional Loving is a
full-time job. There are times when one may regret setting foot on this path, because this awareness does not

necessarily make life easier. It does, however, make life better.

The path of love is not an intellectual exercise. It is living and breathing, a constant challenge, ever changing, always requiring discipline and forethought. If we choose the path of love, we must always walk it. For if we don't, we no longer live life to our potential.

No matter what the situation, no matter what the challenge, we are now called to love without condition. Our very essence, our soul itself, is now committed to the cause.

The Law of Unconditional Loving is a tough taskmaster. Once we taste the fruits of unconditional loving, we cannot go backward, we cannot become "unaware" ever again. We may make a detour or two. We may lose our way. But we cannot release awareness of the power of unconditional loving once it is our own. It becomes ours for all eternity. And it has its demands.

The Law of Unconditional Loving demands first that we see ourselves as spirit. We are co-creators, and through the choice of the spirit of loving, we fashion our lives. Love demands that we create with wisdom. We must keep our thoughts, words, and emotions clear and honest.

The Law of Unconditional Loving demands that we know all the laws of wellness. They are our power tools. The more we know, the more empowered we will become.

The Law of Unconditional Loving is wellness in the most inclusive sense. All the other laws connect through this greatest of laws. Unconditional loving embraces the practical essence of the entire wellness journey.

Loving without condition precludes us from ever blaming again. Blaming serves no purpose. It robs us of the power to change. It has no place in our lives. To blame another is to blame ourselves. Accountability, yes. Blame, no.

Unconditional loving forces us to examine all the artificial barriers in life and discard them. Boundaries between nations, attitudes that maintain that certain people are better than others, even self-concepts of in-dependence—all are obsolete. They have no meaning. They serve only to separate people from one another. The life of unconditional loving has no boundaries. Allegiance belongs to loving itself.

The Law of Unconditional Loving transcends time and space. Love travels in an instant. It crosses all boun-daries, real and perceived. It lasts forever. Love demands that we constantly conduct quality-control checks on ourselves. When we feel that too much negativity is present in our system, we must heal ourselves immedi-ately. Remember, we are the co-creators.

The path of unconditional loving does not lead us through the woods of violence. It demands that we heal our actions, attitudes, words, habits, and thoughts. The law demands that we give up violent politics and

weapons, and all violent human interactions, replacing
them with soul-nurturing counterparts. Swords into
plowshares must become our new commitment.

The Law of Unconditional Loving requires us to re-
lease ourselves from the artificial desires that control our
lives: drugs, alcohol, negative habits, fears — anything
that causes us to lose the capacity to love. We must constantly re-create wellness by releasing our lower wants
and seeking greater levels of spiritual growth.

The Law of Unconditional Loving requires us to
accomplish all this while being gentle with ourselves and
others. A wholesome discipline is what we seek. Loving
through force of will alone, through determination
without compassion, is a form of self-inflicted violence.
Value your wellness. Gently honor yourself.

Unconditional loving demands that we keep our
focus. We must compare ourselves with ourselves — not
with others. In our practice of spiritual growth, our own
commitment to grow in love is the only measure of
progress. Learn to be still and hear the inner voice of
the soul.

Above all, the Law of Unconditional Loving de-
mands that we practice loving. We must do so daily,
hourly, minute by minute. In walking that path, we find
the great joy of the ultimate call and reap the greatest
rewards of wellness.

It's the Law of Unconditional Loving, the highest
of the non-negotiable laws of wellness. Through its

practice, one reaps the great rewards of health, wisdom, and compassion and becomes an instrument of peace.

We need this law today as never before. Many times in our history, the world has been blessed with people of vision, people who could clearly see that the massive amount of suffering in our world is unnecessary. When we see through the eyes of unconditional loving, we will find solutions to our global problems. Then we will discover how to be global beings, sharing one planet, sharing one way of life while honoring our diversity.

May *that* new world order be born. May we all be healed. May we each know wellness and may the planet know wellness. And may we enter the twenty-first century as a global community practicing the Law of Unconditional Loving. That is wellness of the highest order . . . for ourselves and for the generations to come.

More about the work of Greg Anderson

Greg Anderson is co-founder and chairman of The American Wellness Project, which is an effort devoted to the development of total wellness based on many of the ideas in this book. The mission statement of the project reads:

Our mission is to empower people and organizations to enhance their health and enrich their lives through the understanding and practice of total wellness.

This process of empowerment is carried out through seminars and workshops held across the United States. In addition, The American Wellness Project provides on-site development programs for business, health-care, educational, and nonprofit organizations.

The American Wellness Project's products and programs provide a wide range of resources for the empowerment of individuals, families, and organizations.

The American Wellness Project
P.O. Box 238
Hershey, Pennsylvania 17033
1-800-238-6479